W9-AWL-864

—PEOPLE TO KNOW—

JOHN F. KENNEDY

President of the New Frontier

Michael D. Cole

ENSLOW PUBLISHERS, INC.

44 Fadem Road	P.O. Box 38
Box 699	Aldershot
Springfield, N.J. 07081	Hants GU12 6BP
U.S.A.	U.K.

Library of Congress Cataloging-in-Publication Data

Cole, Michael D.
     John F. Kennedy: president of the New Frontier / Michael D. Cole.
        p. cm. — (People to know)
     Includes bibliographical references and index.
     Summary: Presents the personal and public life of the man who came from a
family of wealth and privilege, entered politics, and was elected president at age
forty-three.
     ISBN 0-89490-693-3
     1. Kennedy, John F. (John Fitzgerald), 1917-1963—Juvenile literature.
2. Presidents—United States—Biography—Juvenile literature. [1. Kennedy, John F.
(John Fitzgerald), 1917-1963. 2. Presidents.] I. Title. II. Series.
E842.Z9C65 1996
973.922'092—dc20
    [B]   95-23481
                                                CIP
                                                AC

Printed in the United States of America

10 9 8 7 6 5 4 3 2 1

Illustration Credits:
The John F. Kennedy Library, pp. 11, 13, 17, 26, 30, 34, 36, 41, 69, 73,
75, 78, 85, 87, 96, 100, 106, 109, 111, 112.

Cover Illustration:
The John F. Kennedy Library

Contents

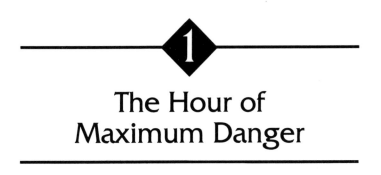

The Hour of
Maximum Danger

The Cold War was growing hotter by the hour.

United States spy planes had discovered Soviet nuclear missile sites under construction on the island of Cuba, just ninety miles off the coast of Florida.

Worse, additional Soviet ships were presently headed toward the newly Communist island. It was possible, even likely, that those ships carried additional missiles and launching equipment.

President John F. Kennedy knew that the situation was gravely serious. With offensive missiles in Cuba, the Soviet Union could launch a quick, short-range nuclear attack on targets in the United States.

On October 22, 1962, President Kennedy announced a naval blockade of all Soviet ships trying to reach Cuba. The Soviet ships were to be stopped and inspected by United States naval troops before being allowed to continue toward Cuba. The stage was set for a confrontation between the world's two nuclear superpowers.

On television, President Kennedy addressed the nation about the newly discovered missile sites. ". . . To halt this offensive buildup," he said, "a strict quarantine of all offensive military equipment under shipment to Cuba is being initiated. . . ."[1] Kennedy called for prompt and immediate withdrawal of all offensive bases on Cuba before the United States would consider lifting the blockade, and he issued a warning:

> . . . it shall be the policy of this nation . . . to regard any nuclear missile launched from Cuba against any nation in the Western Hemisphere as an attack by the Soviet Union on the United States, requiring a full retaliatory response on the Soviet Union. . . .[2]

With Kennedy's words, the line was clearly and dangerously drawn. This was an ultimatum; the Soviet Union must now decide between peace or war. The world waited to see whether the Soviet ships would turn or would steam on toward Cuba and the beginning of a frightening nuclear war.

President John F. Kennedy waited, too.

He had committed himself and his nation to maintain peace in the Western Hemisphere, to defend freedom, and to fight Communist oppression around the world. Strangely, that commitment to peace now had brought about the possibility of a nuclear war that could mean the death of millions. Kennedy had said in his inaugural address a year earlier:

> In the long history of the world, only a few generations have been granted the role of defending freedom in its hour of maximum danger. I do not shrink from this responsibility; I welcome it.[3]

Kennedy's "hour of maximum danger" had come. He had faced crisis and danger before in his life, but now the lives of millions depended on his leadership, his courage, and his humanity. Within a few days he had used these skills to defuse the tensions between the United States and the Soviet Union over the missiles in Cuba, peacefully ending one of the most dangerous situations in history.

He came from the famous Massachusetts Kennedy family—a large, wealthy, Irish-Catholic family. Joseph Kennedy, John F. Kennedy's father, had been everything from a movie producer to a United States ambassador. As a young man, John Kennedy traveled the world and lived a life of privilege. He was not a great student, nor was he very ambitious. Throughout his youth, in fact, it seemed quite unlikely that John Fitzgerald Kennedy, with his fun-loving and leisurely manner, would ever become President of the United States. It seemed unthinkable that he would one day do battle in a war of nerves between the two most powerful nations on Earth.

John F. Kennedy changed over the years, however. He kept his good looks and magnetic charm, but his days of travel and leisure slowly gave way to a life of politics and ambition. He soon assumed the lead in his powerful family, and his successes and victories came quickly. At age forty-three, he became the youngest person ever to be elected President.

John F. Kennedy's life, and his death, would be forever burned into the nation's memory.

His uplifting and tragic story is uniquely American.

The Kennedys
of Massachusetts

Joseph Patrick Kennedy was an ambitious Irish-Catholic man from Boston with a lot to prove. At the heart of real power, he believed, was money, so he went after it, and everything else he sought, with a determination and gusto his children would inherit.

He was president of a Boston bank by the age of twenty-five; he was one of the youngest bank presidents in the country. In 1914, he married Rose Fitzgerald, the daughter of John "Honey Fitz" Fitzgerald, the mayor of Boston. Their first child, Joseph Patrick Kennedy, Jr., was born a year later.

In 1917, Joseph Kennedy, Sr., became assistant general manager of Bethlehem Steel's giant shipyards in Quincy, Massachusetts. On May 29 of that same year,

Joe and Rose's second son, John Fitzgerald Kennedy, was born.

During this time, Joseph Kennedy also earned a small fortune in the stock market, and he pooled his funds with a group of Boston financiers to buy a chain of thirty-one movie theaters in the New England area. He hoped that this success would push him into the world of high finance, but it did not.[1]

At that time, the powerful inner circles of the financial world were not open to a person of Irish descent like Kennedy. The refusal of the financial establishment to accept him pointed the opportunistic Joseph Kennedy toward New York and Hollywood, where motion picture production was evolving. By the late 1920s, Joseph Kennedy had won control of several movie companies, organized them, produced two movies himself, then resold the companies at a huge profit.

His activities in Hollywood and on the stock market were amassing a huge fortune for the growing Kennedy family, which now included Joe, Jr., John, Rosemary, Kathleen, Eunice, Patricia, and Robert. In 1926 Joseph set up a separate trust fund for each of his seven children. By the age of nine, John F. Kennedy probably had a million dollars.

John, who was called Jack by most who knew him, grew up during these years in a three-story house in Brookline, Massachusetts, where he attended Dexter School. Although his older brother, Joe, Jr., was a strapping,

Although he was frail as a youngster, the young boy everyone called "Jack" never shied away from rough-and-tumble activity. Here, at age five, the future President fancies himself as a policeman.

energetic young boy, Jack had many illnesses and struggled almost constantly with his health. He had scarlet fever when he was four years old, and he had several bouts of whooping cough and bronchitis. He was always very thin, and he was born with an unstable back that plagued him throughout his life.

In 1926, the family moved to Riverdale-on-Hudson, near New York City, where Jack attended fourth, fifth, and sixth grades at Riverdale Country Day School. He was popular with his teachers because of his outgoing personality, and he showed a special interest in history.

Jack had a rebellious streak that grew stronger during these years. He resisted the regimented routine his mother made for him and his brothers and sisters. Jack developed a sly, sharp wit; he was quite unlike his more serious siblings. He was almost always late, and gave little attention to his clothes or appearance. Jack simply was more casual than his siblings, and he often appeared rumpled compared to the other Kennedy children. It was all a deliberate effort to be himself, not what his mother wanted him to be.[2]

In 1929, the family moved to Bronxville, New York. They had lived there only a short time when Joseph Kennedy bought a large house in Hyannis Port, Massachusetts. The Kennedys, who now had an eighth child, Jean, soon settled in the Hyannis Port house that became the family home.

That same year, the older Kennedy children were

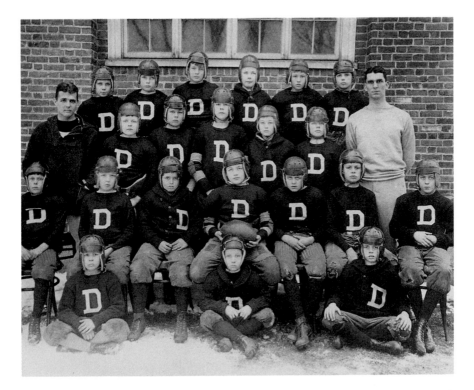

John F. Kennedy attended the elementary grades at the Dexter School in Brookline, Massachusetts. At school, especially in athletics, John was often in the shadow of his older, bigger, and stronger brother Joe, Jr., who is in the second row, third from the left. John is far right on the bottom row.

shipped off to boarding school. Joe, Jr., was sent to the Choate School in Wallingford, Connecticut. Jack would follow him there, but first he spent his seventh grade year at Canterbury, a Catholic prep school in New Milford, Massachusetts.

Canterbury boarding school was Jack's first time away from home. He admitted in letters that he was very homesick, but he quickly grew busy with studies, and he played on the football and field hockey teams. Despite his scrawny physique and unstable back, Jack threw himself into these rough sports with the true Kennedy competitive spirit. "My nose, my leg, and other parts of my anatomy have been risked around so much that it is beginning to be funny . . .," he wrote.[3]

Though Jack soon got over his homesickness, he found the school to be tough and confining. "You have a whole lot of religion and the studies are pretty hard. . . . This place is freezing at night and pretty cold in the daytime," he wrote.[4] He complained about the lack of comfortable clothes and about going to chapel every morning and evening.

Most of all, Jack felt trapped at the school. He had fought against his mother's rules at home in an effort to be himself, but the rules could not be bent or broken at Canterbury, a strict school centered around Catholic religious doctrine. Jack, who greatly enjoyed reading, longed for books or magazines about something other than religion.

He wanted his father to send him issues of a news magazine. "Please send me the *Litary* [sic] *Digest*," he wrote, "because I did not know about the Market Slump until a long time after . . ."[5]

The slump Jack wrote about was an effect of the stock market crash that had wrecked the United States economy in October 1929 and had sent the nation into the Great Depression of the 1930s. Jack's father had seen the crash coming, and had made certain the Kennedy fortune was safe.

Jack was doing well at Canterbury, getting high grades in English, math, and history, but his health was becoming an obstacle to success. He began feeling faint or dizzy often. He was losing weight and had not grown in a year, an unusual thing for a thirteen-year-old boy. As his health began to slide, so did his grades.

His father took him to Palm Beach for Easter, hoping Jack would regain his health and energy in the warm Florida weather. Only a week after he returned to Canterbury, Jack collapsed with appendicitis. His recovery from the emergency surgery was slow, and he fell behind at school. Instead of having him return to Canterbury, the school decided to let him regain his strength at home, where he was tutored until he passed the school exams.

During the summer of 1931, Jack had a new baby brother to play with, the ninth and last of the Kennedy children. Jack had suggested naming him George

Washington Kennedy, since he had been born on Washington's birthday, February 22. Instead he was named Edward Moore Kennedy, after one of Joseph's close friends. The family called him Teddy.

Summer ended, and Jack arrived at Choate School in the fall of 1931. Everyone expected him to follow in the footsteps of his older brother, Joe, Jr., By this time Joe, Jr., was a husky and impressive young man, determined to succeed at everything he tried, as his father had taught him to do from an early age. Joe, Jr., was popular at Choate, and he was motivated by a strong desire to please his father with his accomplishments.[6]

Jack was a little different. While he embraced the proud and competitive Kennedy spirit when it came to sports, he still resisted many of his family's hard-driving attitudes, clinging as well as he could to the individuality he had managed to carve out for himself. The Kennedy parents brought up their children with an emphasis on success and on the idea that because they were Kennedys, they were special.

The Kennedy children were expected to do well. They had been taught by their father that no one cared about a loser. Kennedys were expected to win. In any competition—on their sports teams, in sailing races, or in school—Kennedys were expected to be winners. Even the touch football games the family played at Hyannis Port were quite competitive. Any visitor expecting a leisurely game of football was soon run over by one or

By 1931 the Kennedy family of nine children was enjoying their beachfront home at Hyannisport, Massachusetts. From left to right are Robert, John, Eunice, Jean, Joseph, Rose, Patricia, Kathleen, Joe, Jr., and Rosemary. (Edward is not shown.)

more of the Kennedy children, both the boys and the girls!

Joe, Jr., took this family attitude to heart more than Jack did. The differences between the two boys showed clearly from the very start at Choate School. An early letter to Joseph Kennedy, Sr., from a housemaster at Choate hinted at what was to come: "Jack has a pleasing personality, and is warmly received by all the boys in the house," the housemaster wrote, "but rules bother him a bit."[7]

From "Mucker"
to Author

No one at Choate School during the mid-1930s could say Jack Kennedy was not determined. He was determined to have a good time.

His teachers at the school in Wallingford, Connecticut, all saw that Jack was highly intelligent and was well liked by everyone who knew him. He simply did not apply himself to his studies. He received average grades, occasionally earning high marks in history or English when a subject of particular interest to him was covered. The rest of the time Jack Kennedy was an ornery cutup.

Though he never made the varsity team, Jack threw his skinny body and bad back onto the football field again. He played football in spite of the unavoidable comparisons with his older, bigger, stronger brother, Joe.

He never won a trophy, but he won a lot of respect. One teammate said that Jack was "a tiger on defense."[1]

His coach agreed: "The most burning thing I can remember about Jack was that he was a fighter. . . . You take Joe, he was a real athlete. But Jack made up for what he lacked in athletic ability with his fight."[2]

Jack needed to put more of this fighting Kennedy spirit into his studies. He was forced to go to summer school after failing to pass all his first-year exams at Choate. He eventually passed them, and when he returned to Choate in the fall of 1932, he promised himself that he would never again fail an exam. Beyond that, he had no intention of changing.

While Jack continued to be a challenge for the teachers and headmasters at Choate, Joseph Kennedy was entering national politics in his usual style—through the back door. He had become a strong supporter and fund-raiser for the presidential campaign of the Governor of New York, Franklin D. Roosevelt. Roosevelt won the Democratic nomination, and he won the presidential election in November 1932. Joseph Kennedy had witnessed the making of a President, and learned many lessons that he hoped could one day be put to use.[3]

Roosevelt was sworn in as President in January 1933. A year later Roosevelt returned the favor of Kennedy's support, as Joseph Kennedy fully expected, by naming him the first head of the Securities and Exchange Commission (SEC).

His father's new position did nothing to change Jack's antics at Choate. George St. John, the headmaster at Choate, wrote in a letter to Jack's father:

> Jack has a clever, individualistic mind. It is a harder mind to put in harness than Joe's. . . . When he learns the right place for humor and learns to use his individual way of looking at things as an asset instead of a handicap, his natural gift of an individual outlook and witty expression are going to help him.[4]

Before his father and the school cracked down on him, Jack fell ill again. This time it was serious, and baffling. Again he had lost weight; he was confined to a bed in the school infirmary with flulike symptoms. He grew weaker as the illness continued, and was taken to a hospital in New Haven, Connecticut, where he grew even more sick. His skin became completely covered with hives, leading doctors to believe that Jack might have some unusual blood condition.

By the time the hives subsided and his health slowly returned, Jack had been in the hospital almost a month. He had been very sick with a condition the doctors could not diagnose, and as his recovery gained momentum, one fact was not lost on Jack: His mother had never come to visit him.

Jack never suffered from a lack of advice or

encouragement from his parents and teachers, but there was a definite lack of affection. His mother's absence during his illness confirmed that. He expected his father to be busy, but his mother had no business responsibilities. She was free to travel abroad and relax at Palm Beach, satisfied to have maids and tutors and nannies raise her children. Despite this, she had never made the trip to his hospital bed.[5]

Choate's headmaster dreaded another year of Jack Kennedy and his friends. George St. John said:

> They weren't wicked kids, but they were a nuisance. At one time, it came to the point where I was saying to myself, 'Well, I have two things to do, one to run the school, another to run Jack Kennedy and his friends.'[6]

Jack and his friends, Lemoyne "Lem" Billings, Ralph "Rip" Horton, and ten other boys, formed a secret club. They called it the Muckers' Club, because at chapel meetings Mr. St. John often referred to disobedient troublemaking students as muckers. The very name of the club was an act of outright defiance to the school.

The club's activities eventually caused so many disturbances at the school that St. John considered having the boys expelled. Membership in the club had grown, and its influence among the school's students rivaled that of the official student council. It was like an opposition party in the school, and St. John did not want opposition. When Joseph Kennedy was informed of Jack's antics, the club was immediately disbanded.

The incident had an odd effect on Jack's life. It forced him to cool his funny business, at least for a time, but it also caused Joseph Kennedy to discover some extraordinary things about his second son. He realized that Jack had an intelligent mind of his own, and that there were qualities in his personality which made people want to follow him.[7]

He also learned that Jack was funny and resourceful.[8] Joseph Kennedy liked that. He discovered a newfound admiration and affection for his son, and Jack knew it. His father no longer saw him as a floundering younger brother of Joe, Jr., who was now a model student and football star at Harvard, but as a young man with unusual personal potential.[9]

Jack graduated from Choate in 1935. He was glad to be gone from what he considered a battleground of discipline.[10] With his father's encouragement, he went to England that summer to study at the famed London School of Economics. Again, Jack fell ill before he could attend any of the lectures, and he had to return home. This time he was suffering from jaundice. The illness lasted most of the summer, while his father tried to convince Jack to attend Harvard University in the fall.

Jack wanted to go to Princeton instead, where many of his friends were going, and where he could escape the shadow of his brother Joe. He fell ill again shortly after arriving at Princeton, however, and he suffered through another long stay in the hospital, where doctors were again baffled by his symptoms, which probably were the early symptoms of Addison's Disease, which would not be diagnosed until 1948.

After leaving the hospital, Jack spent the spring and summer recuperating in Palm Beach, Florida, and at a ranch in Arizona. In the meantime, Jack's father managed to convince him to enter Harvard in the fall of 1936.

At Harvard, Jack played junior varsity football, and he fought his worsening back pain, landing a spot on the swimming team. He worked on the college newspaper and was a member of two social clubs. With the exception of those in history and English, his grades were again only average.

In 1937, President Roosevelt named Joseph Kennedy to be the ambassador to the Court of St. James, which meant that he was the United States ambassador to England. He would be ambassador at a critical time in the United States' relations with England. Adolf Hitler had assumed power in Germany, and the Nazi threat was looming large over Europe. The Kennedy family moved to London, and Jack went there for the summer, after finishing his second year of college.

He returned to England the next year, after Harvard granted him the opportunity to spend the second semester of his junior year traveling in Europe. He traveled to France, Spain, Italy, Germany, and Russia, seeing firsthand the gathering storm of aggression in Europe. He reported his observations to his father in an effort to provide him an additional perspective on European tensions.

While writing his senior thesis in 1939, Jack worked in his father's London office. His thesis was entitled "Appeasement at Munich," and it examined England's inaction in the face of growing Nazi aggression. English Prime Minister Neville Chamberlain claimed that he had reached an agreement for "peace in our time" with Hitler at their 1938 conference in Munich. Germany attacked Poland one year later and went on to conquer France in a matter of weeks in May and June 1940. Only the English Channel separated England from Chamberlain's so-called "peaceful" Nazis now occupying France.

It was a fine thesis, but true to his casual nature, Jack had assembled it only with a great deal of help from friends and from people in his father's office. The basic ideas behind the thesis were his, but some of the writing and organization of those ideas was not.[11]

On the strength of his thesis, Jack graduated with honors from Harvard in June 1940. Joseph Kennedy encouraged his son to turn the thesis into a book. Jack agreed, only after getting even more assistance from others. The book was entitled *Why England Slept.*

Joseph Kennedy pulled strings in the New York publishing industry to get the book published. It was not

Because his father was United States ambassador to Great Britain, John F. Kennedy's book *Why England Slept* received a great deal of attention and publicity in the months preceding the United States entry into World War II.

a badly written book, but he still arranged to have the book reviewed well by certain critics, and he bought enough copies of the book himself (storing them in an attic at Hyannis Port) to place the book on the best-seller list.[12]

Jack Kennedy found himself suddenly transformed. The rebellious "mucker" from Choate school was now a Harvard graduate. At the age of twenty-two, through his own hard work and intelligence and his father's powerful influence, he was now a best-selling author.

The Navy and PT 109

The summer of 1940 was an uncertain time for all young men in America. The course the United States would take in the war was unknown. For young men like Jack Kennedy, who had just graduated from college, it was hard to decide what to do next.

He decided to go to Stanford University in the fall, in order to attend graduate classes in business and government, and to take care of his unpredictable health in the warm California sun.

The Germans were bombing London nightly, and Ambassador Joseph Kennedy doubted that England could withstand the Nazi onslaught. He even said so publicly, winning disfavor from the British and from President Roosevelt. The elder Kennedy had to abandon his own secret presidential aspirations in 1940, when

Roosevelt sought nomination for an unprecedented third term as President. Feeling that the nation faced another crisis ahead, voters wished to retain his experienced leadership, and they elected him to a third term.

As his relationship with Roosevelt and with the British deteriorated, Joseph Kennedy resigned from his post in the fall of 1940. He still supported Roosevelt in the election, but he campaigned to keep America out of the war.

Jack Kennedy was growing more handsome and was popular with women students at Stanford. Many women were drawn to his charm and good looks, but at that time the future was too uncertain for him to make a long-term commitment.[1]

Jack Kennedy registered for the draft in October 1940, and during his time at Stanford, he was always aware of events in Europe and of the growing threat of the Japanese in the Pacific.

In July 1941, Joe Kennedy, Jr., enlisted in the United States Navy and began training to become a naval aviator, one of the most elite positions in the military. Taking his older brother's lead, and recognizing the growing certainty that the United States would enter the war, Jack Kennedy enlisted in the Navy in September 1941. Because of Kennedy's poor health, his father had to use his influence in the Navy Department to get him a passing grade on the physical exam.

His family's name and his reputation as a bright student and excellent writer got him assigned to the

Ambassador Joseph Kennedy, Rose, and their nine children gathered for a family portrait in 1940. From left to right are: Joseph, Patricia, John, Jean, Eunice, Robert, Kathleen, Edward, Rosemary, Joe, Jr., and Rose.

Office of Naval Intelligence in Washington, D.C. He gathered and analyzed reports from foreign stations, summarized them, and rewrote them into the office's daily and weekly intelligence bulletins.

While in Washington, Kennedy was interviewed about his book by a *Times-Herald* newspaper reporter named Inga Arvad. Kennedy's sister, Kathleen, was also a reporter at the *Times-Herald* and was Inga Arvad's friend, and the three began seeing each other socially.

Arvad was a beautiful blond Danish woman who could speak and write in four languages. She was as intelligent and charming as Kennedy, and they made an extremely attractive couple.

Unfortunately for Kennedy, Arvad was married to Paul Fejos, a documentary filmmaker. The FBI (Federal Bureau of Investigation) was also watching her day and night; Arvad was suspected of being a Nazi spy.

The Office of Naval Intelligence could not have one of its officers involved with such a person, so Kennedy was transferred out of the Washington office and down to Charleston, South Carolina.

Following the bombing of Pearl Harbor on December 7, 1941, the United States declared war on Germany and Japan. Now that the country was at war, the FBI widened its surveillance of suspected enemy spies. Kennedy and Arvad were forced to go their separate ways.

The FBI continued to watch Arvad's movements for years, but they found no evidence of espionage by her.

Jack Kennedy was tired of watching the war from an office in South Carolina, so he asked his father to get him assigned to sea duty.[2] Joseph Kennedy again asked the Navy to overlook his son's health problems. This was a bit more difficult to arrange this time, because Jack wanted to be assigned to Melville, Rhode Island, for training on the Navy's new PT (power torpedo) boats.

These were small, fast vessels that charged into close range of enemy ships to deliver a torpedo shot. They received a lot of attention early in the war, and their exploits were glamorized much like those of fighter pilots and flying aces. PT boats were tough on the sailors. The boats' high speed and small size made for a particularly rough ride, especially for Jack Kennedy, with his painfully weak back.

Kennedy was a good PT boat skipper—so good, in fact, that he was kept on as an instructor at the training school. This was not at all the sea duty he wanted. The twenty-five-year-old Jack Kennedy was in an adventurous frame of mind.[3] Although he was a young man, he had seen a great deal of the world and he had already seen both the diplomatic and military inner workings of the government. He had never seen any part of Asia or the South Pacific, however, and he had never seen war from the sharp end.

Kennedy got his chance to see both when he was

shipped to the Solomon Islands in early 1943. In March, Lieutenant John F. Kennedy was given command of his own boat, PT 109.

Kennedy was popular with his thirteen crewmates and with the other crews on the island of Tulagi. Johnny Iles, one of his hut mates, said:

> I thought he was a real good officer. . . . His boat was shipshape and his crew was well organized, orderly. . . . He was jolly. He was a fellow who made you feel good to be with—and you would never have known about his personal, privileged life by visiting with him. He was always a genuine person.[4]

". . . Conditions . . . are not bad out here . . ." Kennedy wrote in a letter to his parents. "Rains every day four or five hours—solid rain, everything gets soaked and on my blue uniform a green mold had grown almost one quarter of an inch thick."[5] "We go out on patrol every other night," he wrote, "and work on the boats in the day time."[6] Kennedy slept on a plywood board to help support his increasingly painful back, but his back was soon the least of his worries.

On the night of August 2, 1943, PT 109 and five other PT boats made a night patrol of Blackett Strait, near the island of New Georgia. It was an extremely dark night with no moonlight. Only one of the PT boats had radar, and all were ordered to maintain radio silence except for emergencies. Kennedy's boat was running on only one of

Lt. John F. Kennedy (second from left) in 1942 with three of his PT boat crewmen, from left to right, Barney Ross, Red Fay, and Jim Reed.

its three engines in order to keep its noise to minimum.

Suddenly Kennedy's crewmates spotted the wake of a Japanese destroyer. Kennedy could not gun the boat's engine or it would sputter out, and he could not turn in time. The Japanese destroyer *Amagiri* rammed into the side of PT 109, causing its gas tanks to explode and ripping it nearly in half. Two of Kennedy's crewmates were killed in the explosion. John Kennedy was thrown hard against the side of the cockpit, then fell on his back across the deck. He was sure he was going to be killed.[7]

Kennedy's part of the boat stayed afloat, with four other sailors on board. Six more crewmen were in the water, two of them injured: Charles Harris had a broken leg; Pat McMahon was badly burned and could no longer swim.

The eleven survivors gathered themselves on the floating hulk and waited to be rescued, but no rescue planes were sent out the next morning. The other PT boat crews who had seen the ramming were certain that the crew of the 109 had gone down with the boat or were burned in the fire that followed.

As the boat began to sink, Kennedy and his crew abandoned it, and they swam to a small island about three miles to the southeast. Kennedy towed the injured Pat McMahon by holding the strap of McMahon's life vest in his mouth like a horse's bit. When Kennedy and

Lt. Kennedy, the skipper of PT 109, is shown here in the cockpit of his ill-fated vessel.

the other survivors reached the island, they collapsed on the beach.

Later in the day, Kennedy and his crewmate Barney Ross swam out into Ferguson's Passage in hopes of flagging down a passing PT boat. None ever came, and both men returned to the island, sick with exhaustion.

After two days, all the men swam to an island they called Bird Island, nearer Ferguson's Passage. To relieve their thirst, they cracked open coconuts and drank the juice, which made all of them sick. Later they drank rainwater dripping off leaves during a downpour.

On the fourth day, Kennedy and Ross swam to Nauru Island, even nearer to Ferguson Passage. The people who lived on the island had canoes. Kennedy carved a message into the rough skin of a coconut shell, writing his name and that there were eleven United States sailors alive on Nauru Island. With some effort, Kennedy managed to ask the islanders to use their canoe to bring help. A group of them soon did so.

The next morning Kennedy was awakened by an islander who said to him in perfect English, "I have a message for you, sir."

The message, from a New Zealand infantry patrol on the island of New Georgia, instructed Kennedy to have the canoers paddle him back to their base. Hours later, a PT boat arrived to pick him up at the infantry camp. On the boat were his friends from the naval base.

Someone yelled, "We've got some food for you."

"Thanks." Jack smiled. "I've just had a coconut."[8]

The island people guided the PT boat back to Nauru Island. The PT crew picked up the rest of Kennedy's crew, and they headed back to the naval base.

After six days, the ordeal of PT 109 was over.

The New Oldest Son

An article about PT 109 by John Hersey, published in *The New Yorker* magazine in mid-1944, took Kennedy's crewmate Barney Ross by surprise.

"We'd never gone around saying, hey, did you hear about us?" Ross said. "But suddenly your name's in print and Hersey made you sound like some kind of hero because you saved your own life."[1]

Whether Kennedy and his crewmates were exactly heroic is a matter of opinion. Nevertheless, Kennedy was later awarded the Navy and Marine Corps Medal for his ". . . extremely heroic conduct . . ." which ". . . contributed to the saving of several lives . . ."[2]

Joseph Kennedy made the best of his son's exploit. Through his encouragement, the *New Yorker* article by Hersey was published and later excerpted in *Reader's*

Digest. Many young men were committing similar acts of bravery throughout the war, but because Kennedy happened to be the son of a former ambassador, his six-day adventure was known by readers all over the country.

Kennedy stayed in the Pacific until November 1943, when his back pain finally caused a doctor to have him sent back to the states. In mid-June 1944 he underwent a long overdue spinal disk surgery at New England Baptist Hospital; the surgery did not improve the strength of his back. He was recovering from the surgery at home at Hyannis Port when the Kennedy family received tragic news: On August 12, 1944, Joe, Jr., was killed when the bomber he was flying exploded over England. The news was devastating to Joseph Kennedy. His oldest son was gone.

Rose Kennedy remembered:

> Joe went out on the porch and told the children. . . . They were stunned. He said they must be brave: that's what their brother would want from them. He urged them to go ahead with their plans to race [sailboats] that day and most of them obediently did so. But Jack could not. Instead, for a long time he walked on the beach in front of our house.[3]

Kennedy's despairing father kept to his rooms, but he expected his children to cover up their feelings and to stay busy and active. Kennedy found his family's behavior to be a disturbing form of grieving. He was

Kennedy looked thin in June 1944, as he stood outside of Chelsea
Naval Hospital in Boston. From this hospital he was sent to New
England Baptist Hospital for a long overdue back surgery. The
months of PT boat duty had not been kind to his back.

closest to his sister Kathleen, and was glad of her arrival from England, where she had recently married Lord William Hartington.

Unfortunately the Kennedys' season of tragedy was not over. While Kathleen was still visiting, she received a telegram stating that her husband had been killed. Kathleen returned to England to bury her husband, and she stayed to work with the Red Cross.

During the Christmas holiday of 1944, Jack Kennedy began to sense a change in his relationship with his father.[4] He was considering a career in journalism; he could witness important world events but still live a private life. After the death of Joe, Jr., however, Joseph Kennedy had something else in mind for his son Jack. Ever since the Muckers' Club incident, his father had seen political potential in him. Now he was the eldest son, and Joseph Kennedy began to pressure him into a career in politics.

After many talks with his father, Jack Kennedy began to see the possibilities, but he insisted on spending some time as a journalist. Joseph Kennedy got him a job as a special correspondent, writing articles for the nationwide chain of newspapers owned by the Hearst family. He went to San Francisco to cover the conference in which the United Nations organization was created. In June 1945 he wrote articles from London about the British elections. After that, he went to Potsdam, Germany, to cover the postwar meeting between England's Winston

Churchill, the Soviet Union's Joseph Stalin, and the new United States President, Harry Truman. (President Roosevelt had died in April of 1945.)

Kennedy's articles were not written well. He was a keen observer of world events, but he was not an exceptional writer, and he had few profound insights to offer. He was spending more of his time in the social scene surrounding these events than he was spending on his articles.

This was only further proof that Kennedy's strength was not in his writing skills but in his personality. He had a natural charm that engaged the people he met—a useful quality for a politician. For John F. Kennedy, this was a natural gift that grew even stronger with his age and widening range of experience.

None of this was lost on Joseph Kennedy, who was laying the groundwork for his son back in Boston. He traveled around Massachusetts and organized a team of advisers for a political campaign. Because he was a friend of the secretary of the Navy, Joseph Kennedy had the Navy's destroyer 850 renamed the USS *Joseph P. Kennedy, Jr.* A Veterans of Foreign Wars post in Boston was also set up in Joe, Jr.'s name. After returning from London and after another bout with jaundice, Jack, another Kennedy war hero, became the post's president.

In Boston, the Kennedy name was soon linked with service and sacrifice to the country. John F. Kennedy, only twenty-eight years old, gave in to his father's urging and plunged himself into the risky, challenging life of a politician.

Their target was the congressional seat in Massachusetts' Eleventh District, which included Cambridge, parts of Boston, and several Boston suburbs. In January 1946, Kennedy established his legal residence in the Eleventh District in a room of the Bellevue Hotel, near the Massachusetts State House. His claiming the hotel as his legal residence in the district was an example of the questionable ethics frequently practiced by Jack and Joseph Kennedy throughout Jack's career.

The campaign team decided to run Kennedy as a war hero. Jack Kennedy had gone into the Navy and to war almost immediately after college. He was an author and had written some articles, but he had never held a regular job. His war hero status was the only foundation on which to build an interesting campaign.

As a Democratic candidate for Congress, Kennedy went out to meet the voters. After a few weeks he had developed a knack for walking into restaurants, poolrooms, and taverns to shake hands with dozens of strangers. His ability to mix easily with the public surprised even his father.

The elder Kennedy said:

> I'll never forget the day Jack started his first campaign . . . He walked up to a bunch of hard-boiled guys standing on the corner, put his hand out and introduced himself, asking for their

vote. I remember saying . . . I would have given odds of five thousand to one that this thing we were seeing could never have happened. I never thought Jack had it in him.[5]

Kennedy met and talked to people from all walks of life in the district. He gave hundreds of speeches, walked the streets shaking hands, met workers outside factories, and even went door-to-door, climbing endless flights of stairs in tenement houses. The pace was hard on Kennedy, who was still thin and frail from his always tenuous health.

Not only Jack Kennedy was working hard. This campaign was a Kennedy family effort, and the Eleventh District was overrun by Kennedys. Rose gave several speeches to women's clubs. Eunice, Patricia, and Jean appeared at house parties. Robert, recently home from the Navy, worked three wards in the Cambridge area. Even fourteen-year-old Teddy did odd jobs and ran errands.

The campaign would arrange house parties, sometimes four or five a night, during which Kennedy would talk to twenty people over sandwiches and sodas. He spoke at afternoon teas with Gold Star Mothers—clubs of women who had lost their sons in the war. "I think I know how you mothers feel," Kennedy would tell them, "because my mother is a Gold Star Mother too."[6] The loss of Joe, Jr., gave these mothers a feeling of commonality with Kennedy.

Kennedy's hard work and personal magnetism won

him the Democratic primary election. On June 18, 1946, he beat nine opponents, almost ensuring a general election victory in the highly Democratic district.

"The pros of the district thought of him as a millionaire's son," said campaign adviser David Powers. ". . . they wondered how he could get longshoremen and freight handlers and truck drivers—people who worked hard for a living—to vote for him. He just climbed more stairs and shook more hands and worked harder than all the rest combined, and when they counted the vote, he had received 42 percent of the total votes cast."[7]

In January 1947, the Eleventh District of Massachusetts had a new representative in Congress—twenty-nine-year-old John F. Kennedy.

Representative Kennedy

Kennedy's election to Congress was the beginning of a new career. Being a member of Congress had little appeal to Jack Kennedy, however. He was uninterested in the daily workings of his office, and he lacked the organizational skills to run his Washington, D.C., and Boston offices well. He was very dependent on his staff and on the advice of his father.

Jack Kennedy never completely fit in with his older, shrewder, more experienced colleagues in the House of Representatives. His back pain and several illnesses had left him thin and frail-looking, and he dressed sloppily compared to the other House members.[1] The young representative and future President was often mistaken in the halls for an office boy or an elevator attendant.

Despite his initial discomfort as a House member,

Kennedy was fortunate in his congressional committee assignments. Among them were his appointments to the House Committee on Education and Labor, and to a subcommittee of the House Veterans' Affairs Committee. Both of these committees handled issues that were very important at that time, as troops returned home to work and to raise families in the years immediately following World War II. Still, Kennedy found that he simply was not satisfied with life as a House member.

Kennedy's first term in the House of Representatives was, therefore, undistinguished. His great interest was in foreign affairs, but his position in the House and the nature of his committee assignments kept him far removed from any dealings with foreign policy.

He managed to become somewhat expert on the issues of labor and public housing—the two issues in which he invested most of his energy while in the House. Kennedy also supported federal aid for parochial schools, sought a higher minimum wage and liberalized immigration laws, and supported a broadening of social security—all stances that made him popular with his mostly immigrant Catholic constituents back home. His popularity got him reelected to the House twice: He ran unopposed in 1948, and he clobbered his Republican opponent in 1950.

Kennedy's lackluster career in the House of Representatives was due partly to continuing struggles with his health. In the fall of 1947, he fell ill in London during a congressional trip to study foreign labor problems. A London doctor diagnosed Addison's Disease.

Addison's Disease is a rare condition in which the adrenal glands produce a chronic insufficiency of hormones. Very ill, Kennedy came back to Boston, where the diagnosis was confirmed. The diagnosis of Addison's Disease explained many of Kennedy's previous bouts with jaundice and infection. Among other symptoms, Addison's Disease impairs the body's ability to regulate body metabolism and to fight infection.[2]

Following the diagnosis, he was given daily injections of desoxycorticosterone acetate (DOCA), a synthetic hormone that increased his adrenal hormone activity. After about a month, Kennedy began having DOCA pellets implanted in his thighs every three months, to eliminate the daily need for injections. Because of the fear that public knowledge of Kennedy's health problems would harm his career, the diagnosis and treatment of his disease were kept a secret.

In 1949, in conjunction with DOCA, Kennedy began taking oral doses of cortisone, a newly developed hormone that increased the energy and appetite of Addison's sufferers.

Cortisone changed John F. Kennedy's life. It kept him relatively free from illness for the rest of his life, and it gave him the energy and stamina he had previously lacked. By increasing his appetite, cortisone gave him a level of health he never had before. Kennedy never again looked thin and gaunt. As he grew older, his face and his body filled out for the first time. In his late thirties and early forties he appeared healthier and more handsome than ever before.

This dramatic change in his appearance contributed a great deal to Kennedy's later political appeal, especially with the advent of television.

The DOCA and cortisone treatments, together with a closely controlled diet, would allow an Addison's sufferer to lead a mostly normal life. If the treatments and diet were not closely followed, however, Kennedy could die before he was fifty.

While Kennedy and his family kept a close eye on his newly treatable condition, tragedy visited the Kennedys once more. On May 13, 1948, Jack's favorite sister, Kathleen Hartington, was killed in a plane crash in France. Kennedy took the news of her death very hard, and it caused him more than ever to examine what he was doing with his life.[3]

He realized that he had been unhappily biding his time for years as a congressman. It was time to move on. He and his father decided it was time to take a shot at becoming a United States senator from Massachusetts. In the United States Senate he would have more power and influence, and he would deal more with national issues and matters of foreign policy. Kennedy and his father also knew that the Senate would provide a greater stage from which to display the abilities and accomplishments of a future President.

The race for the Senate would not be easy. The seat was held by a popular Republican, Henry Cabot Lodge, Jr., who had defeated his last Democratic opponent by 330,000 votes. He was a politician at the height of his power.

On April 6, 1952, Kennedy formally announced his candidacy. Oddly, the politics of Kennedy and Lodge differed very little. They both had mixed records of liberalism on domestic issues, and they held similar views on foreign policy, including support for creating the North Atlantic Treaty Organization (NATO) and sending troops to Europe. Both men were vocally anti-Communist.

This race, therefore, would not be a fight over politics or policy. It would be a fight between the Republican and Democratic parties of Massachusetts, but more accurately, a fight between Lodge's Republicans and all of the Kennedys.

By 1952, under Joseph Kennedy's supervision, a Kennedy political campaign had evolved its own structure and strategy independent of the traditional state Democratic Party apparatus. The Kennedy name had acquired a sense of glamour and celebrity in Massachusetts. The arrival of a Kennedy, any Kennedy, at a local campaign function was considered something of an event.

"Rose wowed them everywhere," said Kennedy campaigner David Powers. "They loved her. . . . the family prestige of the Kennedys among the Boston Irish did Jack no harm."[4]

Powers also remembered the other Kennedy women going door-to-door:

> One of the girls would ring a doorbell . . . and say, 'I'm Eunice Kennedy.' The lady of the house would say, 'Oh yes dear! Won't you come in?' Then she'd run into the bedroom and change into a cocktail dress, even though it was only ten o'clock in the morning, and she'd get on the phone and call up four or five neighbors and say to them, 'Guess who's in *my* house? Eunice Kennedy!'[5]

Joseph Kennedy assigned Jack's younger brother Robert, who had just graduated from the University of Virginia Law School, to be the campaign manager. Robert Kennedy proved to be efficient, organized, and fiercely loyal to his brother. He was also developing a political shrewdness that would aid Jack Kennedy in the future.

Bobby, as everyone called him, could also be abrasive and ruthless in the course of doing his job for his brother. These were traits Joseph Kennedy admired in his middle son. "Bobby is like me," the elder Kennedy said, then he described Jack in comparison: "You can trample all over him [Jack], and the next day he's there for you with loving arms. But Bobby's my boy," Joseph added. "When Bobby hates you, you stay hated."[6]

Robert Kennedy believed that the campaign strategy was really very simple:

> The campaign was basically constructed on Congressman Kennedy moving around the state, seeing as many people as possible. . . That's why we held the teas and why we developed the coffee hours and all of the other personal kinds of contact that had never been done before. Because it was so different . . . it received a great deal of attention.[7]

Kennedy never stopped traveling around the state. He shook hands, gave speeches, and attended parties in 351 Massachusetts towns, many of which he visited several times. While the Kennedys were out in force, Lodge was committing mistakes he could not afford to make.

Lodge had been very busy as a prime supporter of Dwight Eisenhower for President, leading up to Eisenhower's nomination at the Republican National Convention. When Lodge returned to Massachusetts late in the summer, he realized that he had been busy campaigning for Eisenhower when he should have been campaigning for himself.

Lodge knew that he was in trouble. Jack Kennedy and his family were blanketing the state.

By the time Lodge knew what he was up against and

had fully mobilized his campaign, it was too late. On a tense election night in November 1952, Henry Cabot Lodge, Jr., was defeated by John F. Kennedy—by seventy thousand votes.

One friend of the Kennedys was not at all surprised that there would soon be a Senator Kennedy. "Poor old Lodge never had a chance," the friend said. "The Kennedys were like a Panzer division mowing down the state."[8]

Jackie and the Senator

In January 1952, Senator John F. Kennedy attended the inaugural ball for the newly-elected President Dwight D. Eisenhower. At Kennedy's side as he entered the ballroom was an attractive young woman named Jacqueline Bouvier.

Kennedy had met Jacqueline Bouvier a year earlier, but his campaign and her trip to Europe had kept them apart for several months. Jackie, as almost everyone called her, was quite different from the women Kennedy had been dating.

Jacqueline Bouvier was twenty-two years old when she met Jack Kennedy. Twelve years younger than Kennedy, she was the daughter of John and Janet Bouvier. John "Black Jack" Bouvier was a stockbroker who had lost his fortune as a result of alcoholism. His drinking and sexual adventures also contributed to a divorce, after which Bouvier's mother, Janet, married Hugh Auchincloss.[1]

Auchincloss was very wealthy from holdings in the Standard Oil Company, and the Auchincloss family wealth made Bouvier part of high society. She attended the prestigious Miss Porter's School in Farmington, Connecticut, and in 1947 she was named Debutante of the Year. She was attractive, intelligent, and cultured, and she traveled extensively, becoming fluent in both French and Spanish.

Bouvier attended Vassar College before receiving a bachelor's degree from George Washington University in 1951, the year she met John F. Kennedy. At that time, she was working as a photojournalist for the *Washington Times-Herald.*

Jackie said:

> It was a very spasmodic courtship, because he spent half of each week in Massachusetts. . . . He'd call me from some oyster bar up there, with a great clinking of coins, to ask me out to the movies the following Wednesday in Washington.[2]

Kennedy loved westerns and Civil War pictures. He was not the candy-and-flowers type, so every now and then Kennedy would give Jackie a book.

Kennedy was definitely not the romantic type. He waited until Bouvier's newspaper sent her to London to cover Queen Elizabeth II's coronation, then proposed to her by telegram.

Bouvier found the Kennedy family to be a rough-and-tumble bunch. Kennedy's sisters made fun of her "babykins" voice and bowled her over in their touch football games. They even made jokes about her large feet, telling her she should give up ballet in favor of soccer.[3] Bouvier said that these first meetings with the Kennedys were like a sorority hazing. She soon understood and accepted that when she married Jack Kennedy, she would marry the whole Kennedy family.[4]

Their wedding, on September 12, 1953, in Newport, Rhode Island, was one of the biggest social events in years. Eight hundred people were present at the ceremony, and twelve hundred attended the reception. Joseph Kennedy planned most of the wedding, a lush Kennedy extravaganza that ensured heavy press coverage.

After a honeymoon in Acapulco, Mexico, the newlyweds returned to Washington, D.C. Kennedy was starting at the bottom again, as a freshman Senator, but the Senate now provided him with the opportunity to speak out on foreign policy. He was very critical of President Eisenhower's inaction against Communists in Southeast Asia. Kennedy insisted that a non-Communist regime in Vietnam would be the key to security in that entire region.

These anti-Communist sentiments of the Cold War reached a new height with the activities of Senator

Joseph McCarthy. By 1954, McCarthy and his Committee on Un-American Activities had accused many prominent government officials of being Communists. The overwhelming majority of the accusations were unfounded, but the anti-Communist fervor in the country was so strong that few dared challenge McCarthy for fear that they too would be branded as Communists.

McCarthy's smear tactics led to a movement by some in the Senate to censure him. The time would soon come when Senator Kennedy would have to voice his opinion on McCarthy's controversial activities. This presented a problem. The Kennedys, who still saw Jack as a potential candidate for the presidency, sought to have him avoid controversial matters such as McCarthy's hearings. Complicating things further was the fact that McCarthy was an old family friend who enjoyed strong support in Massachusetts. He had even dated Kennedy's sister Eunice.[5]

Opposing McCarthy could be harmful at home. Supporting him could be harmful to future national presidential hopes.

Kennedy never had to decide. The reason, once again, was his health. In October 1954, he was admitted to the Hospital for Special Surgery at Cornell University Medical Center. His lower back pain had grown worse in the last two years, to the point where he was forced nearly always to walk with crutches. "I'd rather be dead than spend the rest of my life on crutches," he told his wife.[6] On October 21, 1954, a double-fusion operation was performed on his lower spine to strengthen his back. Because of his Addison's Disease, the operation was very risky. The surgery went well, and at first, Kennedy's condition following the operation was good.

Three days later, as had been feared, infection set in. Kennedy lapsed into a coma. His condition was critical and remained that way for three weeks. More than once the doctors believed he was near death. At one point his condition appeared hopeless, and he was given the Catholic sacrament of last rites.

Jackie Kennedy stayed by his side through it all, gaining the grudging respect of the entire Kennedy family. As the time passed, Jack Kennedy's condition began to improve. He awoke from the coma and regained some of his strength.

During this time, the vote to censure McCarthy was taken. Though Kennedy was awake and capable of communicating his opinion to his aides in Washington, he did not. Though his ordeal in the hospital was unfortunate, he realized it was politically well timed. His illness was a convenient dodge. He escaped going on the record about McCarthy, who was eventually censured by the Senate.[7]

Kennedy stayed in the hospital until the end of December, when doctors decided he could recuperate faster at home. At the family's estate in Palm Beach,

Florida, he rested for another two months while staying in daily contact with his Senate aides in Washington. Then another infection set in, sending him back to the hospital. A second operation removed a metal plate from his spine that was used in the first operation. His condition worsened, and he was again given last rites. Once more, Kennedy fought back and recovered.

He returned to Palm Beach, still in great pain. By early March he was able to walk fifty feet without crutches. Over the following weeks, he gained strength until he was able to walk freely again. There was still pain, but the surgeries had helped enough to allow him to walk without crutches.

In May he returned to his Senate office, where he was greeted by a large basket of fruit and candy from Vice President Richard Nixon, who held the office across the hall. An article in the *New York Herald-Tribune* said, ". . . young Jack Kennedy comes from a bold and sturdy breed, and he's back on the job again."[8] His operation and illness were attributed to injuries he had received during the war.

His suffering, his recovery, and his return to the Senate further added to the public sense of admiration for Kennedy. Consequently, it increased his appeal as a future presidential candidate.

Kennedy's illness yielded yet another unexpected boost to his presidential hopes. Kennedy began work during his recovery on a book about political courage, called *Profiles in Courage.* The volume included biographies of John Quincy Adams, Daniel Webster, and six other Americans who had exhibited courage and commitment to their political ideas. Kennedy formulated the book with the help of his speechwriter, Ted Sorensen, and a host of other accomplished writers and researchers.

The true authorship of *Profiles in Courage* is a subject for debate. Although John F. Kennedy took sole credit as author of the book, it is clear that he did not write it alone. The structure and style of his speechwriter, Ted Sorensen, is evident throughout the book. Although Sorensen denies writing the book, it is almost certain that he wrote it with the research assistance of others. Kennedy's contributions were, at most, the idea for the book, and a few observations about each of the biographies.[9]

Nevertheless, Kennedy's *Profiles in Courage* was published in early 1956 to rave reviews. As with *Why England Slept*, Joseph Kennedy "arranged" many of the good reviews, and engineered a publicity and marketing campaign that ensured the book a place on the best-seller list.

The following year, Kennedy was awarded the Pulitzer Prize for Biography for *Profiles in Courage*. It was an intellectual credit any presidential hopeful would want.

John F. Kennedy was quickly becoming a hot item

in the Democratic party. By August of 1956, the young senator was considered a contender for the vice presidential nomination at the Democratic National Convention. Adlai Stevenson was again the party's presidential nominee, while Kennedy and two Senators from Tennessee, Estes Kefauver and Albert Gore, Sr., were favorites for the running mate position.

Against his father's wishes, Kennedy wanted the vice presidential spot. When Stevenson threw the vice presidential nomination open to the delegates, Robert Kennedy and the Kennedy sisters were mobilized to circulate through the convention and twist delegates' arms. Television covered the political drama, as Kennedy forces ran a tight race with Kefauver's. Finally, when Gore withdrew on the third ballot, Kefauver took the nomination.

Kennedy was greatly disappointed, and he was bitter at Stevenson for throwing the nomination open to the floor, a move he thought showed a lack of judgment and leadership.[10] Still, Kennedy stepped up to the podium and gave his support to Kefauver with grace. The defeat was still a victory for Kennedy's future.

A Kennedy biographer wrote:

> The dramatic race had glued millions to their television sets . . . Kennedy's near-victory and sudden loss, the impression he gave of a clean-cut boy who had done his best and who was accepting defeat with a smile—all this struck at people's hearts in living rooms across the nation.[11]

The Stevenson-Kefauver ticket was clobbered by President Eisenhower and Vice President Nixon in November. Following the Republican victory, Kennedy thought of Joe, Jr., and of the burden of political destiny he had been carrying ever since his brother's death:

> If he had lived, he would have gone on in politics . . . and like me he would have gone for the vice presidential nomination. But unlike me, he wouldn't have been beaten. Joe would have won the nomination . . .

Kennedy separated from the shadow of his brother Joe, Jr., seeing for the first time perhaps, a political destiny of his own:

> . . . and then he and Stevenson would have been beaten by Eisenhower and today Joe's political career would be in shambles and he would be trying to pick up the pieces.[12]

Because of careful planning and a knack for turning even illness and defeat into opportunities, most of the pieces were already in place for John F. Kennedy to have a run at the presidency.

On to the White House

At the end of 1956, Jack Kennedy knew he had four years to become President. Everything appeared ready for the push. He was a rising star in the Democratic party, he had his father's wealth and influence, and the public viewed him as both a war hero and an intellectual.[1]

The Kennedys' presidential hopes for Jack, however, were not without worries. He was young and arguably inexperienced; he was also a Roman Catholic. Because much of the country's population was Protestant, many people did not believe that America was ready to elect a President who was Roman Catholic.

There was one other worry. In the 1950s, a politician's chances for higher office could be ruined by divorce. Increasingly, Jack and Jackie's marriage was strained by his devotion to his career.

Their difficulties reached a peak shortly after the 1956 Democratic Convention. Kennedy went off to the French Riviera to discuss his political future with his father, instead of staying with Jackie, who was to give birth very soon. Jackie had a miscarriage while he was away, and when Jack, who was aboard a yacht, was informed of the sad news, he made no effort to hurry home to comfort his wife.[2]

The incident damaged their marriage, though Jackie insisted there was never any threat of divorce. She accepted Kennedy for his strengths and weaknesses. In much the same way, she disliked politics but stayed committed to Jack's career.[3]

On November 27, 1957, Caroline Bouvier Kennedy was born. This time Jack Kennedy was there. Kennedy was moved emotionally by the birth of his child, and it caused a positive change in him and in his marriage.[4] Still, there was little time for him to concentrate on being a family man.

After his national exposure at the Democratic Convention, hundreds of speaking invitations poured into his office. With Ted Sorensen, Kennedy traveled around the country throughout 1957 giving speeches, meeting people, and making friends with important party leaders. The speeches Sorensen wrote were rousing, eloquent, and occasionally poetic, and Kennedy was greatly improving his skill as a public speaker. Most audiences around the country found Senator Kennedy's speaking engagements impressive.

In 1957, Senate Majority Leader Lyndon Johnson gave Kennedy a coveted seat on the Senate Foreign Relations Committee. The activities of the important, high-profile committee kept Kennedy's name in the headlines, creating the impression of a man experienced in foreign affairs.

Kennedy was also a member of the McClellen Committee, a special Senate committee investigating labor racketeering. Robert Kennedy was the chief legal counsel for the committee. In hearings heavily covered by the press, Jack and Robert Kennedy found themselves going face-to-face with the Teamsters Union president, Jimmy Hoffa, who, the committee showed, had strong links to organized crime. The hearings received a lot of attention, and the public got an almost daily dose of the Kennedy brothers fighting the country's bad guys.

Massachusetts reelected Kennedy to the Senate in 1958. He won more than 73 percent of the vote, the largest majority ever won by any candidate for any office in Massachusetts.

Following the victory, and throughout 1959, Kennedy and Sorensen continued to travel the country, giving speeches and making important allies. As Jack Kennedy physically filled out, and as his speech delivery continued to improve, his image and words made a strong impact on his audiences. Everywhere he went, he drew large crowds. It was obvious to most people at these gatherings that he was planning to run for President. The impression he made, and the image he and Jackie Kennedy created together, seemed perfect for such a race.

On January 2, 1960, John F. Kennedy stated his belief that the country needed a wake-up call, and he formally announced his candidacy for President of the United States. He declared that American science and education lagged behind those of other countries, and that we must find a way "to end or alter the burdensome arms race, where Soviet gains already threaten our very existence."[5]

His speeches were often full of generalities about a lack of direction in the country and a lack of leadership in Washington. The speeches sought to communicate the idea that the country had become stale and unmotivated during the 1950s. Kennedy promised he would "get the country moving again."[6]

Kennedy's only real Democratic challenger was Senator Hubert Humphrey of Minnesota. Kennedy won the first presidential primary in New Hampshire, but the second primary happened to be in Wisconsin, one of Humphrey's neighboring states. The Kennedys sought to beat him badly, knowing a defeat so close to his home would undermine Humphrey as a credible candidate. Trudging through the cold Wisconsin spring was the Kennedy campaign, led by Jack and Robert Kennedy.

Humphrey traveled and made as many speeches as Jack did, but just as in the Massachusetts campaigns, in Wisconsin there were Kennedys everywhere. Where there was not a Kennedy, there was Kennedy money.

Kennedy won the Wisconsin primary, but he did not crush Humphrey as he had hoped to do. In fact, his victory came from winning three heavily Catholic districts, while he lost four predominantly Protestant districts and barely carried the rest that were mixed. He would have to prove his political strength in the next primary in West Virginia, where 95 percent of the people were Protestants.

Kennedy took the religious issue head-on in West Virginia, cleverly tying it to his war record. He said in Morgantown:

> Nobody asked me if I was Catholic when I joined the United States Navy . . . And nobody asked my brother if he was a Catholic or a Protestant before he climbed into an American bomber to fly his last mission.[7]

The Kennedys also spent money on television appearances, posters, bumper stickers, lapel pins, and billboards. Democratic voters in West Virginia saw the smiling image of John F. Kennedy everywhere they looked. Humphrey's campaign could not compete, and because he allowed Kennedy's religion to continue as a main issue in the campaign, a vote for Humphrey began to seem like a vote for religious intolerance.

Senator Kennedy campaigned hard in West Virginia to win a huge victory over his main challenger for the 1960 Democratic presidential nomination, Senator Hubert Humphrey. Humphrey had made religion an issue in the campaign, but Kennedy, a Catholic, still won the primary election in the mostly Protestant state.

The debate over Kennedy's religion eventually backfired for Humphrey. Kennedy defeated him in West Virginia by carrying forty-eight of the state's fifty-five counties. Humphrey was no longer a viable candidate for the nomination. Presidential primaries were not decisive in 1960 in the way they are today, but by the end of May 1960, Kennedy had won seven primaries and was carrying enough popular momentum among party members to be likely to take the nomination by a landslide at the Democratic Convention in Los Angeles.

Just five days before the convention opened in July 1960, Senate Majority Leader Lyndon Johnson announced his own candidacy. He criticized Kennedy's youth and inexperience, in comparison to his own solid legislative record during twenty-three years in Congress. Kennedy's support among the delegates remained strong, however, and he won the nomination on the first ballot.

Kennedy and Johnson did not like each other. Johnson liked Robert Kennedy even less; he considered both of the Kennedys to be rich young upstarts. With Johnson's opinion of them in mind, Robert resisted Jack's argument that he needed Johnson as his vice presidential candidate.[8] Robert Kennedy simply could not abide Lyndon Johnson, but Jack convinced Robert that having Johnson as Vice President would bolster party unity and would give the ticket additional support in the South.

After a period of indecision, Johnson decided to take

the second spot on the ticket. Kennedy gave his acceptance speech and left the July convention as the Democratic candidate for President of the United States. As expected, in August the Republican National Convention nominated Richard Nixon, the current Vice President under President Eisenhower.

Kennedy and Nixon were old friends from their days in the House of Representatives, but they could not stay friends for long. Because the differences in their political ideas were actually minimal, the campaign became a rather personal one in which each candidate sought to convince the country that he possessed better personal qualities of leadership than his opponent.

Because of his more recent exposure at his party convention, Nixon led in the polls. Kennedy hammered away at his opponent, putting Nixon in the position of defending the record of the Eisenhower Administration, which had been popular for the last eight years, but which Kennedy had a talent for portraying as stagnant and uninspired.

America's economy was growing, its position in the world was strong, and most Americans found the 1950s to be a happy time. Despite these facts, Kennedy was able to create the image of an America that was falling behind and wandering aimlessly into an uncertain global future. With his youthful good looks and his war hero and intellectual credentials, he was creating the image of a man who would "get the country moving again."[9]

To Kennedy's huge advantage, the age of televised political imagery had come. A series of debates was scheduled between the two candidates. These were the first presidential debates ever televised. Nixon, who had a reputation as a debater, was expected to defeat the youthful and inexperienced Kennedy easily.

The first debate proved otherwise. Kennedy was cool and confident, and millions watched on television as he carried himself with a handsome and commanding presence. Meanwhile, Nixon seemed a bit shaken and nervous. He was pale, and he looked much older on television than in person. At one point, little beads of sweat appeared on his forehead and upper lip. Kennedy was newly tanned from campaigning in California, and he appeared much healthier and more vigorous than Nixon.

True political differences between the two men were hard to find, but Kennedy's personality and his manner of communication during the debate projected a much stronger impression on television than Nixon did. It appeared to most of the TV audience that the "inexperienced" Kennedy had held his own with Nixon, and many felt that he had beaten Nixon in the debate. It is interesting to note, however, that many who listened to the debate on radio, without the visual imagery of television, thought Nixon had outdone Kennedy.

Nixon did a bit better in the three debates that followed, but Kennedy kept him mostly on the

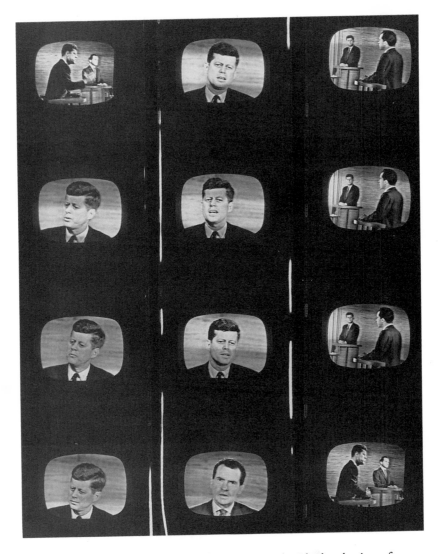

The age of televised political imagery arrived with the election of 1960. In the first televised presidential debates, John F. Kennedy's handsome appearance and confident presence on television gave him an advantage over the less-polished Vice President Richard Nixon.

defensive. At all times Kennedy seemed in command of himself and of the issues, and he appeared utterly at ease with the millions of television viewers around the country.

Kennedy's image of new and vigorous leadership was crucial to his campaign, and now television had magnified it. Following the debates, his campaign took on a new excitement. He began to be swarmed everywhere he appeared. Many of the crowds who greeted him were in a mood of near hysteria, like the excitement that usually greeted a rock-and-roll star rather than a politician. The debates and other television appearances had given him a critical boost.

There was one central reason for the excitement that had ignited the campaign: Candidate John F. Kennedy had charisma, which carried the campaign into the final lap.

Election day was Tuesday, November 8, 1960. That evening, the Kennedys and their campaign strategists gathered in a makeshift headquarters in a room of the Kennedy home in Hyannis Port. The fact that he had been an exciting candidate from the majority political party in the country was balanced by the fact that he was a Roman Catholic and was considered by many to be too young for the office. The election surely was going to be close.

Early in the evening, the CBS network predicted a Kennedy win with 51 percent of the vote. The count

After the televised presidential debates, large and sometimes near-hysterical crowds swarmed to Kennedy's campaign appearances. It was evident that his performance in the debates had given him a huge boost.

stayed close throughout the night, but by late the next morning, it was evident that Kennedy had won, in a squeaker.

Shortly after 11 A.M., Nixon conceded. Kennedy, his family, and his aides piled into a caravan of cars outside the Kennedy home to head toward the Hyannis Armory to meet the media. As the cars began moving, Kennedy's sister Pat noticed that their father was not with them. Kennedy stopped the motorcade and looked back to find his father standing alone on the front porch. He had worked in the background throughout Jack's political career, and apparently chose to stay behind at the house, still in the background.

The new President-elect got out of the car, walked back to the house, and insisted that his father come along to hear his speech.

It was a moment of triumph they had both been working toward for a long time. Kennedy would not allow his father to miss it.[10]

1961 —
The New Frontier

Washington, D.C., was snowy and very cold on the morning of January 20, 1961. Displaying his youthful vigor, the newly sworn-in President John F. Kennedy shed his overcoat to deliver his inaugural address, in which he spoke of a new and bolder America:

> Let every nation know, whether it wishes us well or ill, that we shall pay any price, bear any burden, meet any hardship, support any friend, oppose any foe to assure the survival and the success of liberty.[1]

Kennedy's address echoed his campaign promise that America would stand firm and strong against the Communist influences of the Soviet Union. The President said he and his generation had been granted

On January 20, 1961, forty-three-year-old John F. Kennedy was inaugurated on the east front of the Capitol, becoming the first American President born in the twentieth century. It was a bitterly cold day, but the new President spoke without a coat.

the role ". . . of defending freedom in its hour of maximum danger. I do not shrink from this responsibility; I welcome it."[2]

Defending freedom during the Cold War would not be easy. The Communist struggle for control of Vietnam, the division between democratic West Berlin and Communist East Berlin, and increasingly hostile relations with the newly Communist island of Cuba would all be areas of great concern to the new President.

The civil rights movement was also gaining momentum, and Kennedy tied it to the American push for human rights around the world. In his Inaugural Address he asked the American people to join in a historic effort to ". . . struggle against the common enemies of man: tyranny, poverty, disease and war itself. . . .[3] And so, my fellow Americans," he continued, "ask not what your country can do for you; ask what you can do for your country."[4]

Many Americans, mostly young people, were ready to answer the call, as Kennedy generated a new civic-minded enthusiasm across the nation. This enthusiasm was what Kennedy needed if America was to embark on what he called the New Frontier.

The new President and the First Lady were young and energetic. The handsome couple now had two young children, Caroline and John, Jr., born just after Thanksgiving, who would be running through the White House. Their youthful family image and the glamorous style they brought to the White House attracted the nation's attention and made Kennedy very popular during the first months of his New Frontier.

Kennedy had already weathered the controversial move of nominating his brother Robert as United States attorney general. Some balked at Kennedy nominating his own brother to such an important post, but he believed that Robert's experience as legal counsel in the Senate qualified him for the position. Also, he wanted someone in his presidential cabinet who would always be loyal to him and whom he could unfailingly trust.

On March 1, 1961, Kennedy signed an executive order creating the Peace Corps, an organization that sent American volunteers into developing foreign nations. These Peace Corps volunteers helped teach the people of these nations better agricultural practices, and they helped build bridges, schools, and medical facilities.

The Peace Corps captured the imagination of many young Americans, who put their educations to work for the people of foreign lands. More than five thousand volunteers signed up for the Peace Corps almost immediately. These and other volunteers served in forty-seven countries during Kennedy's presidency.

The introduction of televised presidential press conferences boosted Kennedy's popularity. Kennedy excelled in these question-and-answer sessions, and his easy manner and quick wit helped establish a friendly relationship with the reporters attending the conferences.

President Kennedy also increased surplus food distribution to jobless Americans, and expanded the Food for Peace program to fight hunger in foreign nations. On March 28, 1961, he initiated the largest peacetime military buildup in United States history. Kennedy increased a number of nuclear missile programs and ordered five additional combat divisions. In response to growing tensions in Laos and Vietnam, he ordered a 400 percent increase in the number of antiguerilla forces.

On March 13, he had also announced the establishment of the Alliance for Progress, an aid program aimed at promoting economic development and political reform in Latin America. This program sought to improve conditions in that region and to decrease the threat of revolutionary movements, specifically Communist ones like that of Fidel Castro, who had taken over Cuba in 1958. Castro's regime was aided greatly by the Soviet Union, which succeeded in making Castro's Cuba the first Communist government in the Western Hemisphere.

In April 1961, Cuba became an embarrassment to Kennedy. Just five days after the Soviets had beaten the United States to Kennedy's much-wanted goal of putting the first human in space, an attempted United States invasion of Cuba turned into a horrible disaster.

The invasion plan was left over from the Eisenhower Administration, which had severed diplomatic ties with Cuba just days before Kennedy took office. A group of

Cuban exiles in the United States had been trained for an invasion, and by April they were ready to make the attack. The plan assumed that the invasion would incite rebellion among dissatisfied Cubans, who would then join and assist the invaders in overthrowing Castro.[5]

The entire invasion was planned to appear as if the United States had not been involved. It was to appear instead that the Cuban exiles had bought military equipment from the United States and had enlisted only limited assistance from United States military advisers.[6]

On April 17, 1961, the Cuban exiles landed at the Bay of Pigs on the southern shore of Cuba, but the air cover from old United States bomber planes was insufficient to protect the invaders, who were pinned down on shore. No uprising by the people of Cuba took place, nor would it have taken place if the invasion had gone well. Prior to the invasion, nearly all of Castro's enemies were dead, or in jail, or had escaped from Cuba. Most of the fourteen hundred United States-trained Cuban invaders who landed on the island were captured or killed.

Kennedy had been leery of the invasion from the beginning, but the new President had trusted the knowledge and experience of his advisers in the military and the CIA (Central Intelligence Agency) over his own political instincts and military experience.[7]

His instincts proved right. The invasion was a total disaster, and United States involvement in the invasion could not be hidden or denied. Castro and Soviet leader Nikita Khrushchev condemned the United States for the underhanded attack.

The failed invasion was a huge blow to the Kennedy Administration. The Soviet's recent space triumph, followed by a botched United States-inspired invasion of a rather small island, made Kennedy's people look like a second-rate operation in the eyes of the world. The New Frontier looked like a joke.

Kennedy was angry with his advisers and was upset by the aftermath of the invasion.[8] He took total responsibility for the Bay of Pigs fiasco. This harsh lesson taught him to question more fully the recommendations of his advisers. He would never again mistrust his own instincts.[9]

On May 5, 1961, America's space program got its first small victory when Alan Shepard became the first American in space. On May 25, Kennedy proposed to Congress a new space effort designed to put an American on the Moon before the end of the 1960s. Success in space flight would win political prestige around the world for the country that triumphed. Kennedy wanted to beat the Soviet Union to the Moon. The Space Race was now fully under way.

On May 31, 1961, President and Mrs. Kennedy flew to Paris, France, where they were greeted by President Charles de Gaulle. Jackie Kennedy spoke fluent French, and the enthusiastic French people who lined the streets everywhere the couple traveled were utterly charmed by her. At a large dinner gathering, President Kennedy introduced himself as "the man who accompanied Jacqueline Kennedy to Paris . . ."[10]

Three days later Kennedy flew to Vienna, Austria, for his first meeting with Soviet Premier Nikita Khrushchev. The two discussed Laos and Vietnam, the tensions in the divided city of Communist East Berlin and democratic West Berlin, as well as future prospects for nuclear disarmament.

Clearly the Soviet leader sought to intimidate the young President, who was still politically shaken from his failure in Cuba. Khrushchev took a hard line on Berlin. Both countries had troops in the city, but because Berlin was situated inside Communist East Germany, nearly four thousand refugees were fleeing from East Berlin into democratic West Berlin every week. Seeking to stop this exodus, Khrushchev told Kennedy that he would sign a separate peace treaty with East Germany, making all of Berlin part of Communist East Germany. Khrushchev demanded that United States troops be removed from West Berlin by the time the treaty was signed.

Kennedy told Khrushchev that he would fight if United States access to Berlin was cut off. Khrushchev responded that he would meet force with force.

"Mr. Chairman," Kennedy said in his last words to Khrushchev, "it's going to be a cold winter."[11]

When the President and First Lady arrived for a visit to France in June 1961, enthusiastic crowds treated the young and glamorous couple like visiting royalty.

The threat of war hung over the Berlin situation, and Kennedy left the Vienna summit discouraged with United States-Soviet relations.[12]

In a television address upon his return to the United States, Kennedy described his meetings with Khrushchev as somber. Kennedy told the nation that he and Khrushchev:

> ... have wholly different views of right and wrong, of what is an internal affair and what is aggression, and, above all, we have wholly different concepts of where the world is and where it is going.[13]

While the Berlin crisis brewed through the summer of 1961, Kennedy signed a bill to extend social security benefits to several million Americans, permitting them to retire with benefits at age sixty-two. He approved the Housing Act, an area redevelopment measure that aided communities with chronic unemployment problems. Kennedy also signed bills to fight water pollution and to create a series of national seashore parks, as well as the Wheat and Feed Grain Bill, designed to increase farm income and to lower food surpluses.

In mid-August 1961, the Berlin crisis reached its height, as East German troops closed off all crossing points between East and West Berlin. Roadblocks were set up, and a wall of barbed wire was constructed. Days later, cinder blocks, concrete, and mortar were trucked in, and construction of the Berlin Wall began.

Kennedy sent fifteen hundred troops across the East

Kennedy's meeting in Vienna with Soviet Premier Khrushchev in June 1961 was a tense and ultimately negative confrontation between the two leaders. Khrushchev's threats about West Berlin worsened an already dangerous situation.

German border; they moved one hundred and ten miles down the main road toward West Berlin. The troops and tanks took up positions facing Soviet forces on the other side of the border dividing the city. On the last Sunday of August 1961, the Soviet tanks withdrew. The Berlin Wall was completed.

With the completion of the Berlin Wall, the crisis cooled for the moment. The Soviets announced that they would resume atmospheric testing of nuclear weapons. Kennedy responded the next year by announcing that the United States would resume nuclear weapons testing in the Pacific.

In September 1961, Kennedy signed the Minimum Wage Bill, which raised the minimum wage to $1.25 and expanded its coverage to several million workers. In an address before the United Nations, President Kennedy challenged the Soviet Union to a "peace race" and voiced his support for nuclear disarmament. Peace was elusive in the Cold War, however. In December 1961, while seeking peace and improved relations with the Soviet Union, Kennedy pledged increased United States assistance to the South Vietnamese in fighting the Communist North Vietnamese.

Four days after President Kennedy's action on Vietnam, Joseph Kennedy suffered a severe stroke that left the right side of his body paralyzed and rendered him unable to speak. His mind was still reasonably sharp, but his affliction had immobilized him and made communication a struggle. This left the Kennedy patriarch often depressed.[14]

His father's stroke was a sad ending to a tough year for John F. Kennedy. "Even if my dad had only ten percent of his brain working, I'd still feel he had more sense than anyone else. . . ." Kennedy later said.[15]

As 1961 drew to a close, Kennedy faced something he had not yet experienced in his presidency or in his life: He would not have the help of his father. Joseph Kennedy, the architect of past Kennedy successes, was now disabled. He could no longer offer advice and exert influence over his sons as he had in the past. This was a new and uncomfortable experience for Kennedy.[16] Problems and tensions around the world were mounting, and John F. Kennedy, for the first time in his life, was on his own.

1962 —
A Year of Crisis

With the influence of his father greatly diminished, President Kennedy now depended even more on his brother Robert.

Robert Kennedy's role in the Kennedy White House changed rapidly in 1962, as his work began to encompass far more than his regular duties as attorney general. He became Jack Kennedy's shadow, his personal informant, and his troubleshooter in any problem area of the administration. It was soon evident to everyone in the White House that Bobby Kennedy was the President's right-hand man.

Vice President Johnson noticed the development with some displeasure. "Every time they have a conference don't kid anybody about who is the top adviser," Johnson said. "It's not McNamara [Secretary of

Defense Robert McNamara], the Chiefs of Staff, or anyone else like that. Bobby is first in, last out. And Bobby is the boy he listens to."[1]

Robert Kennedy was not popular with everyone in the White House, but he was an immense help to Jack Kennedy in keeping the cabinet members and other White House officials in line with his brother's goals. The Kennedy presidency enjoyed a much greater level of success because of Robert's disciplined and vigilant efforts throughout the many executive departments.

President Kennedy's earlier boost to the space program resulted in a major United States space triumph in February 1962, when Colonel John Glenn became the first American to orbit Earth in his Mercury capsule *Friendship 7.* The seven Mercury astronauts were popular and exciting figures to Americans, and they appeared often in public with the President, who enjoyed the special shine they gave to his political image of a New Frontier.

In April 1962 a crisis occurred when the U.S. Steel Corporation announced an immediate increase of six dollars a ton in the price of steel. Kennedy had met earlier in the year with members of the steel industry and the United Steelworkers Union, who had agreed with the President on a much lower steel price. This agreement was part of Kennedy's coordinated economic effort to hold down the nation's rate of inflation.

U.S. Steel was accused of violating that agreement,

and the President was forced to take action against the corporation. Kennedy applied heavy pressure, including threats of investigations into the steel industry for antitrust violations and price-fixing. As a result of the pressure, U.S. Steel eventually backed down, and the price was lowered. The steel crisis was the first episode in which President Kennedy showed his ability to react swiftly and with resolve.

An even more delicate matter awaited him in September. In 1954 the Supreme Court had ordered the desegregation of public schools. Because prejudice does not die suddenly with the passage of law, desegregation did not happen overnight. Many areas of the South resisted the legal desegregation of schools and of public places like bathrooms and restaurants. This southern resistance reached a flashpoint during Kennedy's presidency.

In 1961, an African-American student named James Meredith had applied for admission to the University of Mississippi, which had never before accepted African Americans. When Meredith was denied admission, he filed a lawsuit, and a federal appeals court ruled that he be allowed to enroll at the university. Mississippi Governor Ross Barnett resisted the court's decision, and when Meredith attempted to enroll, he was met by crowds of angry demonstrators and by Governor Barnett himself.[2]

Attorney General Robert Kennedy issued a court

order that Meredith be allowed to enroll. In order to avoid conflict, it was arranged that Meredith would register on September 30, 1962, a Sunday night when the campus would be empty. Thinking that all was proceeding as planned, the President announced on television that Meredith had peacefully entered the campus. But during the speech, Barnett's state troopers allowed an angry mob onto the campus, where a riot took place between the mob and federal marshals. The marshals were forced to use tear gas to protect themselves and Meredith from being massacred at the hands of the rioters, who were armed with clubs and bricks.

Two deaths and many serious injuries resulted from the riot, which forced Kennedy to send in National Guard troops the following day. On October 1, 1962, James Meredith finally enrolled at the University of Mississippi. A year later, a similar drama would again unfold at another southern university, but with less violence.

This incident was a tense way to begin October 1962, which would prove to be one of the most frightening months the world had ever seen. President John F. Kennedy's ultimate test of leadership was about to take place.

Fidel Castro's Communist Cuba lay only ninety miles off the coast of Florida. The greatest threat presented by a Communist Cuba was that Castro might allow the Soviets to place nuclear missiles on the island.

From that nearby base in the Western Hemisphere, Soviet nuclear missiles could be launched against targets all over the eastern United States.

Despite repeated assurances by the Soviet Union that they would never ship nuclear weapons to Cuba, aerial photographs in mid-October 1962 showed indisputable evidence that at least half a dozen nuclear missile launching sites were under construction on the island. On the morning of October 16, 1962, Kennedy was told the news and was shown the photographs. The Cuban Missile Crisis had begun.

President Kennedy immediately assembled a group of his closest advisers, including members of the military, the CIA, and other government departments. The group was called ExCom (Executive Committee of the National Security Council) and was assigned the task of formulating a response to the situation. Kennedy attended the group's first meetings and witnessed the debate between military leaders who supported bombing the missile sites or invading Cuba, and others who supported the idea of a naval blockade of the island.

Kennedy then put his brother Robert in charge of ExCom. The President wanted to keep his regular schedule and to avoid the appearance that something was wrong. He stuck to his travel plans, while staying in regular contact with Robert. The press soon realized that something important was happening, however.

The United States military was in a state of alert, and

the Strategic Air Command put planes in the sky around the clock. It was clear that the United States nuclear defense system had been ordered to a high level of readiness, but no one knew why.[3]

ExCom, meanwhile, was still divided between military action and a blockade. When Robert Kennedy informed his brother of the stalemate, President Kennedy announced he had a cold and was returning from Chicago to Washington.

Upon his arrival, he immediately met with ExCom. There were dangers from all sides in this situation. Inaction would seem like weakness in the face of Soviet aggression. Bombing the launch sites or invading Cuba could get many American troops killed and could escalate the situation into further confrontations with the Soviet Union.

A naval blockade of Cuba could also escalate into wider conflict, but it was less likely to do so than an air strike or invasion. Kennedy felt that the presence of the missile sites would give the United States justification in the eyes of the United Nations for a blockade of Cuba. In the face of a naval "quarantine," as Kennedy called the blockade, it would be the Soviets who provoked any possible confrontations.

A decision was needed quickly. Several missiles already on the island were believed to have a range of eleven hundred nautical miles. They were capable of hitting Washington, D.C., Cape Canaveral, Dallas,

President Kennedy and ExCom, the special committee formed to monitor and respond to the Missile Crisis in Cuba, meets on October 29, 1962. The President and this committee performed with intelligence and firmness throughout the crisis.

St. Louis, and everything in between, including the Strategic Air Command Bases in the region. They could be operational within days.

Losing no more time, Kennedy made his decision and ordered the naval blockade of Cuba. On October 22, 1962, he went on radio and television to brief the nation on the crisis at hand and on the steps he was taking to deal with it. His speech was brief and to the point. He explained that Soviet ships would be stopped, boarded, and inspected for offensive nuclear missile equipment before being allowed to continue toward Cuba.

He called on Khrushchev "to halt and eliminate this clandestine, reckless and provocative threat to world peace and to stable relations between our two nations."[4] Kennedy pointed out the necessary but unavoidable dangers of the blockade, and explained that a bolder, more violent move against Cuba was not yet in the best interests of America or the world. He said:

> The path we have chosen for the present is full of hazards, as all paths are . . . But it is the one most consistent with our character and courage as a nation and our commitments around the world. The cost of freedom is always high—but Americans have always paid it. And one path we shall never choose, and that is the path of surrender or submission.[5]

Two days later, sixty-three ships moved into place around Cuba to enforce the quarantine. At 10 A.M. on October 24, reports came to the White House that two

Russian ships were steaming toward the quarantine line. As the first Soviet ship drew closer to a United States destroyer, word came that a Soviet submarine had moved into position between the two ships.

This was "the hour of maximum danger" the President had described in his Inaugural Address. If the Soviets pushed too far, he would be forced into ordering an attack on the Russian ships, or Cuba, or both, which could result in a rapidly widening conflict that would almost certainly include an exchange of nuclear strikes.

John F. Kennedy knew that he was on the brink of World War III, an insane conflict that potentially could bring about the end of the world. He had pledged to defend freedom around the globe, and now he had drawn his line of freedom in the waters around Cuba. Soviet nuclear missiles would not be tolerated in the Western Hemisphere, and crossing the blockade line to deliver more missiles would be considered an act of war. President Kennedy left the fateful decision about peace or war, coexistence or nuclear annihilation, to Nikita Khrushchev.[6]

President Kennedy, his brother Robert, their advisers, their families, the nation, and the world waited through the most dangerous moment in recorded history. President Kennedy stood firm as he waited, feeling the immense burden of his office.[7] Never before had a President been thrust into such a crisis, where moment to moment the lives of millions hung so precariously on his delicate skills of leadership and diplomacy.

The next report came: At 10:25 A.M. President Kennedy was informed that the Soviet ships near the quarantine line had stopped dead in the water. Minutes later, another message reported that the ships were turning around, retreating from the blockade. The wily Khrushchev had proven himself to be reckless but rational.[8]

The crisis continued for another three days. Some Russian noncombat ships allowed themselves to be boarded and inspected before heading onward to Cuba. Meanwhile, Soviet warships kept themselves at a safe and reasonable distance from the quarantine line. As the crisis began to recede, one relieved ExCom member said, "We're eyeball to eyeball and I think the other fellow just blinked."[9]

President Kennedy had stood tall in his "moment of maximum danger." He had once again shown the Kennedy toughness that had allowed him to prevail over so many other challenges during his life. This time the nation and the entire world had benefited from his toughness. Perhaps appropriately, the first United States destroyer to make contact with the Russian ships had been the USS *Joseph P. Kennedy, Jr.*

Khrushchev later agreed to remove the missiles and the missile sites from Cuba, in conjunction with the removal of some United States missiles from Turkey, near the southwestern border of the Soviet Union. The removal of the United States missiles from Turkey was

The scene of one of many Soviet ship inspections conducted by the
United States Navy quarantine during the Cuban Missile Crisis.

not made public; neither was Kennedy's secret promise to Khrushchev that he would not try to invade Cuba again.

The outcome of the Cuban Missile Crisis was a personal and political victory for Kennedy. His stature as a world leader grew, and he enjoyed support and praise from the American press for his performance during the crisis. The most dangerous episode in the Cold War had challenged his political skills to the limit and had lifted him to the high point of his presidency.

It had also changed Kennedy. During the past year, he had been making an effort to spend more time with Jackie and his family, becoming emotionally involved in his children's lives. This connection to his children, and the thought that there were millions like them around the world, had affected him during the crisis. Those feelings helped make crystal-clear to him the utter insanity of nuclear war, and led him to choose the blockade over the more risky bombing or invasion of Cuba.[10] In the year that remained of his presidency and his life, nuclear disarmament became a primary goal of John F. Kennedy.

Many other challenges still loomed on the horizon. The civil rights movement continued to meet angry opposition in the South. Berlin remained a hot spot. Cuba was still Communist. After two years in office, Kennedy now brought a new confidence to dealing with these problems.

As 1962 ended, John F. Kennedy seemed to have hit his stride as a President.

The End of Camelot

Style and grace still described the Kennedy White House as 1963 began. A chatty year-end television interview in December 1962 had brought the President closer than ever to the American people, much as Franklin Roosevelt's "fireside chats" on the radio had done in the 1930s. Then, as the new year began, came the news that Mrs. Kennedy was pregnant once again.

The youth, high culture, and grand style that the Kennedys brought to the White House led some to call it Camelot—from the musical popular at the time, about King Arthur and the Knights of the Round Table. No one imagined that before the year was over, Camelot would come to a sudden and shocking end.

Hopes were high as the year began. In March, Kennedy urged final action on a Constitutional

Amendment to outlaw the poll tax as a strategy to bar African Americans from voting. This measure would eventually become the Twenty-fourth Amendment.

The last of the Mercury astronauts, Gordon Cooper, flew into space in May. On June 10, the President gave a stirring speech on peace and nuclear disarmament at American University in Washington, D.C. This important speech outlined Kennedy's hopes for a new and more peaceful relationship with the Soviet Union:

> Let us examine our attitude toward peace itself. . . . Too many of us think it is impossible. Too many think it unreal. But that is a dangerous, defeatist belief. It leads to the conclusion that war is inevitable—that mankind is doomed—that we are gripped by forces we cannot control.
>
> We need not accept that view. . . . No problem of human destiny is beyond human beings. Man's reason and spirit have often solved the seemingly unsolvable—and we believe they can do it again.[1]

The next day, the President was again forced to call in National Guard units to assist in the enrollment of two African-American students, this time at the University of Alabama. During the turmoil surrounding the students' enrollment, President Kennedy paused that evening to deliver a major address to the nation on the subject of civil rights:

> We are confronted primarily with a moral issue. . . . The heart of the question is whether all Americans are to be afforded equal rights and equal

opportunities, whether we are going to treat our fellow Americans as we want to be treated.

If an American, because his skin is dark, . . . cannot enjoy the full and free life which all of us want, then who among us would be content to have the color of his skin changed and stand in his place?

One hundred years of delay have passed since President Lincoln freed the slaves, yet their heirs, their grandsons, are not fully free. . . . And this nation, for all its hopes and all its boasts, will not be fully free until all its citizens are free.

Now the time has come for this nation to fulfill its promise. . . . It is a time to act in Congress, in your state and local legislative body, and, above all, in all of our daily lives.[2]

On June 22, Kennedy proposed to Congress the most sweeping civil rights legislation in history. Following Kennedy's death, with the strong support and commitment of President Lyndon Johnson, the Civil Rights Bill would later be passed in 1964.

Two days later Kennedy traveled to West Berlin. A huge throng greeted the President to hear a dramatic speech, which he delivered from a high podium in view of the Berlin Wall. The sight of the Wall and the crowds who hated it unsettled Kennedy, who added to his speech some angry and unplanned words of his own.

"There are some who say in Europe and elsewhere, 'We can work with Communists,'" he said. "Let them come to Berlin!"[3] Later in the speech, Kennedy brought the crowd to a wild roar when he said, "Today in the world of freedom, the proudest boast is, 'Ich bin ein Berliner!'" [I am a Berliner].[4]

At about the same time, negotiations were begun between the United States and the Soviet Union on a nuclear test ban. Kennedy spoke of the test ban, as well as plans for United States-Soviet cooperation in space, in an address before the United Nations. His growing commitment to the cause of nuclear disarmament further enhanced his reputation as a peacemaker and a statesman.

Sadly, the President and Mrs. Kennedy's third baby, Patrick Bouvier Kennedy, was born prematurely. Weighing only four pounds, the baby was unable to survive, and he died three days later, on August 9, 1963. Kennedy was deeply saddened by the loss of the child.[5] Coping with the tragedy brought Jack and Jackie closer together. At the beginning of his marriage, Kennedy was a far cry from the perfect family man. After ten years, and after some very tough times, Jack was finally coming into his own as a husband and a father.[6]

The work of the presidency would not wait for his grief to pass. In August 1963, African Americans showed their support for the Civil Rights Bill by organizing a March on Washington. More than two hundred thousand African Americans and other citizens gathered around the Lincoln Memorial in the largest civil rights demonstration in American history. Dr. Martin Luther

A huge crowd in West Berlin watched as President Kennedy stepped to the podium to deliver a speech within earshot of the newly constructed Berlin Wall. He brought the crowd to a feverish pitch by uttering "Ich bin ein Berliner" (I am a Berliner).

King, Jr.'s stirring "I Have a Dream" speech was the highlight of the day-long demonstration. The march sent a signal to Kennedy, to Congress, and to the rest of the nation that the time for civil rights legislation had come.

The Nuclear Test Ban Treaty with the Soviet Union, signed on October 7, 1963, was the first disarmament agreement of the nuclear age. This victory in the cause of peace came less than a year after the Cuban Missile Crisis.

Although Kennedy was taking a new look at the Cold War and at ways to settle it, his desire to assist the South Vietnamese became a growing problem. The Communist North continued to apply pressure on South Vietnam, and Kennedy was again faced with the possibility of defending peace and freedom in the region only by assisting South Vietnam in war. In 1963, Kennedy renewed and expanded the American military commitment to South Vietnam.

Kennedy then signed a bill that launched the first national effort to render assistance in the areas of mental illness and mental retardation. He also began plans for political trips designed to strengthen his support in the upcoming 1964 reelection campaign. One important place where his popularity needed a boost was Texas, where the Democratic Party was also in the midst of a squabble between factions.

The travel plans to Texas included proposed visits to the cities of San Antonio, Houston, Fort Worth, and Dallas. The people in those cities included groups of

Cubans unhappy with Kennedy's policy toward Castro, racists angry with his support for civil rights legislation, and those who believed that he was either too soft or too harsh on Communism.

The trip was planned for November, and when the time came for the trip, the President took Mrs. Kennedy and Vice President Johnson along—Johnson because he was a native Texan, and Jackie Kennedy for the additional excitement she created during such visits.

The entourage was greeted by enthusiastic crowds in San Antonio, Houston, and Fort Worth on November 21. So far the Texas visit appeared to be a great success.

On November 22, 1963, following a morning speech outside his Fort Worth hotel, Kennedy and his group boarded Air Force One for the short flight to Dallas, where they were met by a cheering crowd of nearly four thousand at Love Field. The President and Mrs. Kennedy shook dozens of hands before stepping into an open limousine with Texas Governor John Connally and his wife.

Cheering people lined the Dallas streets along the motorcade route. The motorcade progressed down Main Street nearing Dealy Plaza. At 1:30 P.M., the limousine took a sharp left turn onto Elm Street and passed the Texas School Book Depository.

Moments later, shots rang out.

A bullet hit Kennedy in the throat; he suddenly clutched at his neck. Governor Connally was also shot

On November 22, 1963, the streets of Dallas were decorated and the crowds were friendly as the presidential motorcade passed by. There was no rain in the forecast, so the President rode in an open car.

through the back, perhaps by the same bullet. Seconds later, another bullet struck Kennedy in the head. Mrs. Kennedy tried to escape the hail of bullets, but a Secret Service agent forced her back into her seat as the limousine raced away toward Parkland Hospital.[7]

The President's heart continued beating for almost another thirty minutes, but the massive head wound from the assassin's bullet had already brought John F. Kennedy's conscious life to an end.

News of the shooting interrupted television and radio broadcasts, and when word came that the President had been pronounced dead, the nation experienced a state of shock unlike any it had ever known. Those who heard the announcement would always remember where they were when they learned John F. Kennedy had been assassinated.

Later that day, Lee Harvey Oswald was arrested and was later charged with the murder of the President, as well as the murder of a police officer he apparently shot because he feared he was being followed.

Two days later, a shocked nation watched on television as Oswald was escorted from city to county jail, and was shot to death by Dallas nightclub owner Jack Ruby.

Conspiracy theories abound about Oswald's role in an assassination plot by Castro, the Mafia, the CIA, the Soviets, and various combinations of these. Such theories have never been proven and probably never will. Lee Harvey Oswald took the answers with him to his grave.[8]

The President and Mrs. Kennedy in November 1963, just nine days before his fateful trip to Dallas.

The First Lady, the Kennedy family, and a mourning nation say farewell to the tragically fallen President.

The Warren Commission, which investigated the assassination, released its final report in September 1964. The Commission, headed by Chief Justice Earl Warren, found no evidence of a conspiracy. The report characterized Oswald as a crazed loner who acted alone in shooting the President from the sixth-floor window of the Texas School Book Depository.[9]

The report was not a perfect piece of investigating. It left many holes open to curious speculation. Many Americans do not totally accept the conclusions of the Warren Commission report, and they have been speculating ever since.

On Monday, November 24, 1963, Americans watched John F. Kennedy's stately funeral on national television. The slow funeral procession and the black-veiled face of Jacqueline Kennedy burned unforgettable images into the collective memory of a mourning nation.

Perhaps the most memorable image is that of young John F. Kennedy, Jr. At his mother's urging, John, Jr., stepped forward and gave his father, the President, the old skipper of PT 109, a final military salute. The small boy was too young to comprehend the horror of what had happened, too young to understand his father's hopes for the future.

It was his third birthday.

The Kennedy Legacy

Less than three years after his inauguration, John F. Kennedy's presidency was violently cut short. In those three years, however, he accomplished many things and made an important impact on the presidency and the nation.

At home, Kennedy had expanded public housing and welfare programs for the poor, modernized agricultural policy, and opened new national parks. He moved to protect water and other natural resources, and he supported the development of a number of urban renewal programs designed to help improve the lives of people living in large cities.

Around the world, Kennedy's legacy includes his establishment of the Peace Corps and his fine example of diplomatic leadership for future Presidents, in bringing about the first treaty on nuclear arms, the Nuclear Test Ban Treaty.

Although he did not manage to pass such a dramatic piece of legislation through Congress during his time in office, Kennedy's support for civil rights legislation contributed greatly to the eventual passage of the Civil Rights Bill in 1964.

These are a few of the ideas or creations of the Kennedy presidency that are still with us in some form today. But one of the most important qualities of the Kennedy presidency was Jack Kennedy's own personal style as President.

He and Mrs. Kennedy brought to the White House a level of personal and cultural charm that caught the attention of Americans in the early 1960s. By his telling Americans to "ask not what your country can do for you; Ask what you can do for your country," many Americans felt that their President was pushing himself to his highest level of personal excellence, and asking them to do the same in a civic-minded call to duty. Many answered that call to his New Frontier.

Kennedy's presidency was much too short to accomplish many of the high-minded goals he had described in his Inaugural Address. For many Americans who were alive in the early 1960s, it is the sense of hope for the future that Kennedy created that they most remember about his presidency.

John F. Kennedy described his desire for peace with

the Soviet Union in a speech on nuclear disarmament at American University on June 10, 1963. In that speech, he also spoke some basic truths he might have wanted his children and future generations to know. Kennedy said:

> . . . In the final analysis our most basic common link is that we all inhabit this small planet. We all breathe the same air. We all cherish our children's future.
>
> And we are all mortal.[1]

Chronology

1917—Born in Brookline, Massachusetts.

1922—Attends Dexter School in Brookline.
-1926

1926—Attends Riverdale Country Day School in New
-1929   York City.

1930—Attends and graduates from Choate School in
-1935   Wallingford, Connecticut.

1935—Attends Harvard University, and spends second
-1939   semester of junior year working in his father's
      London office.

1940—Graduates from Harvard with B.S. degree;
      senior thesis published in book form as *Why
      England Slept.*

1941—Enlists in United States Navy.

1943—Commands PT 109 in the Pacific; is decorated
      for acts of bravery after the 109 was sunk.

1944—Brother Joseph Kennedy, Jr., killed in plane
      explosion over Europe.

1945—Writes articles on world affairs as a newspaper
      correspondent for the International News
      Service.

1946—Elected to Congress from the Eleventh District
      in Massachusetts.

1948—Sister Kathleen killed in plane crash in France.

1952—Defeats Henry Cabot Lodge to become United
      States senator from Massachusetts.

1953—Marries Jacqueline Bouvier.

1956—Publishes *Profiles in Courage*; defeated in vice-presidential bid at Democratic National Convention.

1957—Senate hearings on labor racketeering; receives Pulitzer Prize for *Profiles in Courage*; daughter, Caroline, born on November 27.

1958—Reelected to Senate by one million votes.

1960—Announces campaign for presidency; receives Democratic nomination; takes part in four television debates with Richard Nixon; elected 35th President of the United States; son, John F. Kennedy, Jr., born.

1961—Presidential inauguration; establishes Peace Corps; announces Alliance For Progress; initiates large peacetime defense buildup; disastrous attack on Cuba at Bay of Pigs; proposes space program to put an American on the Moon by the end of the decade; meets Nikita Khrushchev in Vienna; the Berlin crisis; renews American commitment to South Vietnam.

1962—Steel crisis; signs public welfare expansion legislation; enrollment of James Meredith at the University of Mississippi; Cuban missile crisis.

1963—Speech on world peace at American University; mobilizes Alabama National Guard to admit two African-American students to the University of Alabama; proposes major civil rights legislation; speech at Berlin Wall; March on Washington; Nuclear Test Ban Treaty signed; assassination in Dallas on November 22.

Chapter Notes

Chapter 1

1. Goddard Lieberson, ed., *John Fitzgerald Kennedy . . . As We Remember Him* (New York: Atheneum, 1965), p. 168.

2. Ibid.

3. John F. Kennedy, Inaugural Address (Washington, D.C.: Government Printing Office, 1961).

Chapter 2

1. James MacGregor Burns, *John Kennedy: A Political Profile* (New York: Harcourt, Brace, 1960), pp. 15–16.

2. Nigel Hamilton, *JFK: Reckless Youth* (New York: Random House, 1992), p. 85.

3. Ibid., p. 86.

4. Ibid., p. 85.

5. Herbert S. Parmet, *Jack: The Struggles of John F. Kennedy* (New York: Dial Press, 1980), p. 28.

6. Peter Collier and David Horowitz, *The Kennedys: An American Drama* (New York: Summit Books, 1984), pp. 59–61.

7. Hamilton, p. 89.

Chapter 3

1. Goddard Lieberson, ed., *John Fitzgerald Kennedy . . . As We Remember Him* (New York: Atheneum, 1965), p. 13.

2. Herbert S. Parmet, *Jack: The Struggles of John F. Kennedy* (New York: Dial Press, 1980), p. 33.

3. Nigel Hamilton, *JFK: Reckless Youth* (New York: Random House, 1992), p. 97.

4. Joan Blair and Clay Blair, Jr., *The Search for JFK* (New York: Berkley, 1976), p. 22.

5. Hamilton, p. 105.

6. Lieberson, p. 17.

7. Hamilton, p. 128.

8. Ibid., pp. 127–128.

9. Blair, p. 30.

10. Hamilton, p. 135.

11. Thomas C. Reeves, *A Question of Character: A Life of John F. Kennedy* (New York: Free Press, 1991), pp. 48–49.

12. Ibid., pp. 49–50.

Chapter 4

1. Joan Blair and Clay Blair, Jr., *The Search for JFK* (New York: Berkley, 1976), pp. 95–96.

2. Peter Collier and David Horowitz, *The Kennedys: An American Drama* (New York: Summit Books, 1984), p. 124.

3. Thomas C. Reeves, *A Question of Character: A Life of John F. Kennedy* (New York: Free Press, 1991), pp. 58–60.

4. Nigel Hamilton, *JFK: Reckless Youth* (New York: Random House, 1992), p. 542.

5. Ibid., p. 534.

6. Ibid.

7. James MacGregor Burns, *John Kennedy: A Political Profile* (New York: Harcourt, Brace, 1960), pp. 48–49.

8. Hamilton, p. 599.

Chapter 5

1. Thomas C. Reeves, *A Question of Character: A Life of John F. Kennedy* (New York: Free Press, 1991), p. 67.

2. Goddard Lieberson, ed., *John Fitzgerald Kennedy . . . As We Remember Him* (New York: Atheneum, 1965), p. 45.

3. Nigel Hamilton, *JFK: Reckless Youth* (New York: Random House, 1992), p. 662.

4. Peter Collier and David Horowitz, *The Kennedys: An American Drama* (New York: Summit Books, 1984), p. 145.

5. Lieberson, p. 48.

6. Ibid.

7. Ibid., p. 49.

Chapter 6

1. Herbert S. Parmet, *Jack: The Struggles of John F. Kennedy* (New York: Dial Press, 1980), p. 170.

2. Joan Blair and Clay Blair, Jr., *The Search for JFK* (New York: Berkley, 1976), pp. 560–566.

3. Peter Collier and David Horowitz, *The Kennedys: An American Drama* (New York: Summit Books, 1984), pp. 171–172.

4. Goddard Lieberson, ed., *John Fitzgerald Kennedy . . . As We Remember Him* (New York: Atheneum, 1965), p. 54.

5. Ibid.

6. Thomas C. Reeves, *A Question of Character: A Life of John F. Kennedy* (New York: Free Press, 1991), p. 102.

7. Lieberson, p. 59.

8. Ibid., p. 55.

Chapter 7

1. C. David Heymann, *A Woman Named Jackie* (New York: Lyle Stuart, 1989), pp. 34–54.

2. James MacGregor Burns, *John Kennedy: A Political Profile* (New York: Harcourt, Brace, 1960), pp. 127–128.

3. Heymann, p. 116.

4. Ibid., p. 115.

5. Peter Collier and David Horowitz, *The Kennedys: An American Drama* (New York: Summit Books, 1984), p. 159.

6. Heymann, p. 170.

7. Herbert S. Parmet, *Jack: The Struggles of John F. Kennedy* (New York: Dial Press, 1980), p. 310.

8. Ibid., pp. 315–316.

9. Thomas C. Reeves, *A Question of Character: A Life of John F. Kennedy* (New York: Free Press, 1991), pp. 127–128.

10. Collier and Horowitz, pp. 208–209.

11. Burns, p. 190.

12. Collier and Horowitz, p. 210.

Chapter 8

1. Gerald S. and Deborah H. Strober, *"Let Us Begin Anew": An Oral History of the Kennedy Presidency* (New York: HarperCollins, 1993), pp. 1–2.

2. C. David Heymann, *A Woman Named Jackie* (New York: Lyle Stuart, 1989), pp. 189–191.

3. Ibid., pp. 193–195.

4. Doris Kearns Goodwin, *The Fitzgeralds and the Kennedys: An American Saga* (New York: Simon & Schuster, 1987), p. 793.

5. Thomas C. Reeves, *A Question of Character: A Life of John F. Kennedy* (New York: Free Press, 1991), p. 158.

6. Peter Collier and David Horowitz, *The Kennedys: An American Drama* (New York: Summit Books, 1984), p. 244.

7. Reeves, p. 162.

8. Collier and Horowitz, pp. 241–243.

9. Ibid., p. 244.

10. Rose Fitzgerald Kennedy, *Times to Remember* (Garden City, N.Y.: Doubleday & Co., 1974), p. 377.

Chapter 9

1. John F. Kennedy, Inaugural Address (Washington, D.C.: Government Printing Office, 1961).

2. Ibid.

3. Ibid.

4. Ibid.

5. Pierre Salinger, *With Kennedy* (Garden City, N.Y.: Doubleday & Co., 1966), pp. 146–147.

6. Ibid.

7. Goddard Lieberson, ed., *John Fitzgerald Kennedy . . . As We Remember Him* (New York: Atheneum, 1965), p. 129.

8. Peter Collier and David Horowitz, *The Kennedys: An American Drama* (New York: Summit Books, 1984), p. 271.

9. Lieberson, p. 129.

10. C. David Heymann, *A Woman Named Jackie* (New York: Lyle Stuart, 1989), p. 302.

11. Lieberson, p. 139.

12. Collier and Horowitz, p. 277.

13. Lieberson, p. 141.

14. Collier and Horowitz, pp. 286–288.

15. Thomas C. Reeves, *A Question of Character: A Life of John F. Kennedy* (New York: Free Press, 1991), p. 313.

16. Ibid., p. 314.

Chapter 10

1. Peter Collier and David Horowitz, *The Kennedys: An American Drama* (New York: Summit Books, 1984), p. 289.

2. Goddard Lieberson, ed., *John Fitzgerald Kennedy . . . As We Remember Him* (New York: Atheneum, 1965), p. 163.

3. Thomas C. Reeves, *A Question of Character: A Life of John F. Kennedy* (New York: Free Press, 1991), pp. 376–377.

4. Ibid., p. 378.

5. Ibid.

6. Gerald S. and Deborah H. Strober, *"Let Us Begin Anew" An Oral History of the Kennedy Presidency* (New York: HarperCollins, 1993), pp. 393–395.

7. Ibid.

8. Robert F. Kennedy, *Thirteen Days: A Memoir of the Cuban Missile Crisis* (New York: W.W. Norton & Co., Inc., 1969), p. 71.

9. Ibid.

10. Reeves, pp. 391–394.

Chapter 11

1. Goddard Lieberson, ed., *John Fitzgerald Kennedy . . . As We Remember Him* (New York: Atheneum, 1965), p. 193.

2. Ibid., p. 197.

3. Ibid., p. 200.

4. Ibid.

5. Kenneth P. O'Donnell and David F. Powers, *"Johnny We Hardly Knew Ye"* (Boston: Little, Brown & Co., 1972), pp. 375–378.

6. Ibid.

7. C. David Heyman, *A Woman Named Jackie* (New York: Lyle Stuart, 1989), pp. 399–402.

8. Bob Callahan, *Who Shot JFK? A Guide to the Major Conspiracy Theories* (New York: Simon & Schuster, 1993), pp. 147–149.

9. Ibid.

Chapter 12

1. Goddard Lieberson, ed., *John Fitzgerald Kennedy . . . As We Remember Him* (New York: Atheneum, 1965), p. 194.

Further Reading

Bishop, Jim. *A Day in the Life of President Kennedy.* New York: Random House, 1964.

Collier, Peter, and David Horowitz. *The Kennedys: An American Drama.* New York: Summit Books, 1984.

Graves, Charles P. *John F. Kennedy: New Frontiersman.* New York: Chelsea House, 1992.

Mills, Judie. *John F. Kennedy.* New York: Franklin Watts, 1980.

Reeves, Richard. *President Kennedy: Profile of Power.* New York: Simon & Schuster, 1993.

Reeves, Thomas C. *A Question of Character: A Life of John F. Kennedy.* New York: Free Press, 1991.

Index

McClellen Committee, 66
Meredith, James, 92, 93

N
New Frontier, 79, 80, 83, 115
Nixon, Richard, 60, 63, 71, 72

O
Oswald, Lee Harvey, 110, 113

P
Peace Corps, 80, 114
Powers, David, 46, 52
PT boats, 32
PT 109, 33, 35, 38, 39

R
Roosevelt, Franklin D., 20,
        24, 28, 29, 102
Ross, Barney, 37, 39
Ruby, Jack, 110

S
Shepard, Alan, 83
Sorensen, Ted, 61, 65, 66
Space Race, 83
St. John, George, 21, 22
Stalin, Joseph, 43
Stevenson, Adlai, 62, 63

T
Truman, Harry S., 43

V
Vietnam, 81, 88, 107

W
Warren Commission, 113

18.95

B-KENNEDY-C
Cole, Michael D
John F. Kennedy.